If You Beat Your Fish It Will Die

If You Beat Your Fish It Will Die

Ray Owens
Joke A Day
www.jokeaday.com

Joke A Day, Inc.
Published By Joke A Day, Inc.

http://www.jokeaday.com

Library of Congress Cataloging-In-Publication Data
Owens, Ray
If You Beat Your Fish It Will Die / Ray Owens

ISBN 0-9750152-0-4 (grade: alk. Paper)

First Edition: December 1999

What's the difference between meat and fish?

If you beat your fish, it will die.

*To those Angels who make **me** laugh:*

Spud
Peanut
Ruhchel Bear

And, of course, Mama and Daddy

Acknowledgements and Thanks!

I could not have put this together without the assistance of many people. (Well, I could have, but the results would have been scary.)

An "I Owe You Big" to Betty Bryant for her tremendous attention to detail and ability to tell me to "piss off" if I didn't like her suggested corrections.

Thanks to my crack (cracked?) proofreaders who reminded me on a daily basis that I had no business making fun of anyone's spelling errors and grammar: Darren Meahl, Finster Paul, Al Hedstrom, Frank Zimmanck, Scott Bechtel, Mark Rider, Robert Cutler, Ryan Tucker, Tom Elliot, and Alex R. Cohen. What I love about you guys is that you work for less than I do! (Do I really need to say that standard "Any error in here is mine" bullshit? Naw, let's blame it on the proofreaders this time! heh heh heh.)

A special thank you to Dr. Mark Fischer. Without a doubt, no human being on the planet knows more jokes than Mark. His mailings to me have pulled my ass out of the fire more than once. God help me if Mark ever decides to start his own humor mailing list -- I'm screwed!

To Vince Sabio, who helped me out with patience and good humor, when I ran just a wee joke list. Best damned list moderator on the planet (except for me!)

And my greatest appreciation to April. The person who has to put up with my bullshit on a daily basis and still wants to have sex with me regularly. I couldn't have done it without you, Love.

Introduction

Welcome to *If You Beat Your Fish It Will Die,* the first book of stuff taken from my website, Joke A Day (www.jokeaday.com).

My name is Ray Owens and I started Joke A Day in January 1997. I'm writing this little introduction mainly for those of you who've picked this book up and have never been to my site or are not a member of my daily email list.

I'd like to invite you to stop by Joke A Day's website and take a look around. I've worked hard over the last few years to provide folks with one thing: a laugh. I hope you'll get more than just one laugh from your visit.

Have you got an email account? Then drop a line to join@jokeaday.com, and I'll get you subscribed to a *free* service where I'll send you some mail every day -- again in the elusive goal of making you laugh.

You're not going to be familiar with my Judi Awards or my Dweeb Letters and you may scratch your head in puzzlement at the letters that are in this book. One of the most amazing aspects of the Internet and my business is the instant communication from the folks who stop by to visit. Some of the communication will make you worry for the future of mankind.

There are lots of dirty words in here. There are lots of people demonstrating how stupid they are. (Hell, even *me!*) But most of all, there are lots of laughs. I hope you enjoy this book!

Ray Owens
Joke A Day

Well, now that we're here, what do we do?

It was Aunt Minta Bee's typewriter that caused all of this.

When I was about seven, I got to spend a few weeks with my Aunt Minta Bee in Bastrop, Louisiana. Aunt Minta Bee worked at the draft board. When I got dropped off at her office, she let me play with a typewriter.

It was one of those old, ancient, manual things. Not electric. Word processors were decades away. (OK, two decades away, but still.) No, it was one of those that you had to have the arm muscles of Charles Atlas (right, "Ah-nold" was also decades away) to type anything faster than 30 words a minute.

Aunt Minta Bee suggested I sit down and play with it. So I did. There I discovered the magic of the printed word.

What was cool was to sit there and write things. Thoughts that were in my head. And see them come to life on that piece of paper behind that noisy damned machine.

Oh sure, I'd sat down and written stuff in longhand before. But penmanship was never one of my strong suits. Plus, after 10 to 20 pages, your hands get tired. (Now I have to worry about carpal tunnel syndrome, but I digress.)

But these were words on paper printed by a machine. Good God Almighty, but I was in hog heaven. *(I wonder how much it had to do with the fact that Clark Kent made his living by typing? Ahhh, the times I remember when Clark was late on a deadline so he'd simply type about 138,000 words a minute. I think he actually melted a typewriter once!)*

The most exciting part of study hall in high school was watching the teacher/monitor fall asleep with his finger in his nose. Instead of enjoying the show, I decided to do a little "self-study" in the typing lab.

The only "formal" typing course I took was in the 9th grade. But I really practiced for three more years. I just never went to study hall.

It was cool being in the typing lab. For one thing, that's where all the "babes" were. Guys were too "cool" to be caught dead typing. (It was us "Bill Gates" types in the lab.) For another thing, I didn't have to pay attention to the teacher. I wasn't in her class to *learn* anything -- I was there to play around (and look up Cindy Bomar's dress).

But the best part was I got to use one of only two electric typewriters in the whole school.

Love notes. Stories. Things I'd love to do to Ruth Reilly (the lady, who, for the missing of a phone call, could have been my bride -- a story for another time). My stories were all about my friends and I used to make us "say" all kinds of funny things in the stories.

And I got pretty good at that typing thing. I never went back to the manual typewriters. *(For one thing, my fingers'd get stuck between the keys now. Doesn't happen on an IBM Selectric II, mind you.) But I was faster than almost anyone in the class. (Yeah, yeah, I was cheating -- they were using manual machines and I was using an electric one, so sue me.)*

Great Lakes, Illinois. United States Navy Boot Camp. June, 1977.

I was always amazed at the number of folks who joined the Navy and could not swim. That has nothing to do with this book, but you'll find me doing this from time to time in here. Just rambling about shit.

In recruit training we had to fill out these silly-assed cards that asked us what special talents, if any, we had. I put down that I could type 60 words per minute. So, it wasn't long after the gathering of those little cards that I was ordered to "lay to" (I'm in my nautical speak mode, y'all) to the Company Commander's office. There I was asked, "Owens, you say you can type?" "Yes, SIR!" "60 words a minute, huh?" "Yes, SIR."

So, they gave me a test to type. And they directed me under the ladder (that's stairs, landlubbers) to where Uncle Sam had stashed his state-of-the-art machine.

And there it was. In all its glory.

The typewriter from Aunt Minta Bee's office.

It made sense. Aunt Minta Bee worked in the draft board. When they abolished the draft, they had all this excess equipment that they didn't need anymore. So it wound up in Great Lakes, for crying out loud.

And I was about to try and type 60 words a minute on the damned thing.

I have to tell you, the results were horrible. I think I managed more like 5 words a minute. With no erasers, or whiteout or correction fluid, there were more mistakes than not.

The Company Commander looked at the pitiful excuse for a document that I handed to him. He looked at me. Shrugged. "Well, Owens, you did better than anyone else did. You're the new Battalion Yeoman."

Being Battalion Yeoman was a perk and a half, let me tell you. Why? Because in the middle of gawd-awful recruit-level exercises (like learning how to make your bunk 25 times in a row) all I had to do was say, "I'm going to go sort the mail," and I'd get out of having to do that silly-assed shit.

I could write myself passes to go anywhere I wanted on base. I didn't have to march in formation nor did I have to go to chow at the same time anyone else did. I was a free man. Well, as free as you can get in recruit training. It wasn't like I could write myself a chit for a girl or something. (But, then again, I never really tried, so who the hell knows what I could have accomplished.)

I was responsible for putting out the Battalion's Plan of the Day. The Battalion Command actually appreciated it when I'd stick a "Humorous Thought of the Day" at the bottom of each one.

Thanks to the typewriter and my ability to type, I "got out of" boot camp. Now, I wouldn't have had as easy a time with boot camp had I also not had three years of Navy Junior ROTC while in high school. While everyone else was learning how to distinguish an ensign from a captain from a master chief, I had that stuff down cold. I knew how to march. I knew my manual of arms. Boot camp was an eight week "get in shape" which I wish today, 22 years later, I could go back and repeat just to get my fat ass back in shape.

Let's recap: My ability to type allowed me to never have to sit through a "study hall" in high school. And now it was making life much easier in boot camp. My typing skill was reaping rewards out the ying-yang.

Patrol Squadron 93.   Selfridge Air National Guard Base.   Mt. Clemens, Michigan.

My first duty station in Uncle's Big Canoe Club.   I was a Personnelman. I'd been to "A" school in Meridian, Mississippi. They pretty much figured out I wasn't going to be able to sink any of our ships on my own, so they graduated me and sent me to another commanding officer. I'm sure they breathed a sigh of relief.

One day the yeoman who was in charge of printing up the "Recall Bill" (a list of names, addresses, and phone numbers of reservists to call to active duty in case the Russians starting doing some shit) came to make me an offer I couldn't refuse. Since he outranked me, there was little I could do about the offer.

But this one was a pretty cool offer. I was going to get to learn how to use a computer.

And, you guessed it. It was Aunt Minta Bee's typewriter again.

No, not really. But it wasn't far removed from it.

It was an old "punch card" operation. Each member on the "Recall Bill" had two cards. The first one was the name and address and the second one was the phone number. When someone had a change to his recall information, you pulled his cards, and marked the changes right on the cards. When you got time to sit in front of the computer again, you pulled all of those changed cards and entered the new information.

But not the way you'd do it today. No, no.

You inserted a new card. And you typed. Did I mention there was nothing to watch while you typed? No monitor. You were typing blind. When you got done typing the new card, you flipped a switch. And the computer kicked out the 80 characters you'd typed in there, punched on that little card. Then you looked at the printed top of the card to make sure what you typed matched what you wanted to type.

After you got done with all of the cards, you manually put them back in alphabetical order and you drove over to the Air Force (which always had better computers than the Navy) and asked them to put it in their big punch card processing computer. A couple of days later, you went over and picked up reports printed on that wonderful computer green bar paper.

I was in love. Here was a machine that could type faster than I could!

A few months later, because I was the guy who "knew the computer," I was given the chance to learn a new computer personnel system. You have to remember this was about 1979/1980. MS-DOS? Forget about it. Windows? Yeah, right. There *was* no operating system. All of the computer manufacturers and software makers had to make their own operating system.

The system was called CADO. It was the Antichrist of programs. After a while we used to just say, "CADO is a four-letter word." (Guess you had to be there.)

My favorite things were those wonderful single-sided seven-inch floppies. A report that listed all hundred people in the command in alphabetical order would take *two hours* to alphabetize and print out.

But that was still faster than I could do it.

Somehow I got the reputation for being the "guy who knows stuff about computers." In reality, I was dumber than a box of rocks.

TEAM America. Columbus, Ohio. 1992

Because I was the only person in the company who could tell you what an "autoexec.bat" file was, the "powers that be" in the company decided I was the best candidate to run their new software. The new software ran under Unix. There isn't an autoexec.bat file on Unix.

"Eunuchs? Are those guys with their dicks chopped off?"

(There was a time when four of my coworkers went to a seminar about "Workplace Dynamics" or some such bullshit. One exercise they had to complete as a group was to identify certain personality types in an office. The moderator would say a type, "Office Gossip" and they'd all write down the name of the person who first came to mind. When they'd gone through just about everything on the moderator's list, they heard, "Office Clown." According to all four of these folks, they took great delight in looking at each other and saying, "Ray Owens." Hardee har har.)

The "powers that be" were religious fanatics and didn't take to my well-thought-out interrogatives about Unix.

Ahh well, they were stuck, too. So they made me their MIS Director, stuck me in a closet, and said, "Learn this Unix thing and make our company grow."

Thank God for *Unix for Dummies*.

Somehow I muddled through it. Somehow I learned enough to prevent myself from being too dangerous. And somehow the company prospered despite it all.

PayPlus Software. Columbus, Ohio. 1994 - 1998.

The software that TEAM America wanted me to work with was from a little company in San Bernardino, California. The president of that company, one of my best friends in all the world, Barclay Bourdeau, had patiently taught me what I needed to know about Unix and his software.

One day, he offered me a job. I think it was because I used to dial into his system and leave jokes in everyone's mailboxes.

The great part about it was that I was going to get to work at home. My basement became my office. It was quite a crew. Me, my fat ass, and my typing ability all in that little space. I used to kid folks about having to be at work at 8:00 a.m. So I'd get up at 7:55 to beat the rush on the stairs.

About 1996 was when the World Wide Web exploded. PayPlus decided that they needed a web page. Because of my typing ability (heh -- that's stretching it, ain't it?) I was chosen to be the fella to create this thing.

Again, thank God for *HTML for Dummies*.

Joke A Day. January 1997.

An Evil Conglomerate company in New Jersey had bought PayPlus. They didn't quite know what the hell to do with me. Everyone in California came to work in an office. Everyone in New Jersey came to work in three piece suits with the obligatory corncob up his ass. But this guy in *Ohio*, for crying out loud, comes to work naked and works out of his home!

Fortunately for me, PayPlus had given me some stock options before the Evil Conglomerate came to town. I made about $22,000 on the deal. I paid off some bills, bought my then-wife a car. (That was *so* cool to be able to go in and pay *cash* for a car. Never done it before then and odds are I won't ever be able to do it again, but it was *cool*.) This got me thinking that no one had ever had the idea of sending jokes via email to people. Why not start up a company based on that very idea?

What a moron I was.

"That idea will never work!" "You can't make any money sending jokes in the email!" "You're doomed to fail!"

(And, if you read the letters throughout this book, you'll see that there are plenty of folks who still feel that way about me -- "what a morcn.")

You're holding proof of my "failure" in your hands.

My ability to type had gotten me out of study hall and boot camp. It led me to a life-long love of computers. (Only women are more interesting to me than computers.) By a series of accidents and lucky breaks, and my love of making people laugh, the stars in the heavens all got together and said, "Ehhh, what the hell. It's only jokes."

Thanks, Aunt Minta Bee.

Ray Owens
Joke A Day

"Once there was a beautiful woman . . ."

Once there was a beautiful woman who loved to work in her vegetable garden, but no matter what she did, she couldn't get her tomatoes to ripen.

Admiring her neighbor's garden, which had beautiful, bright red tomatoes, she went one day and inquired of him his secret. "It's really quite simple. Twice each day, in the morning and in the evening, I expose myself in front of the tomatoes and they turn red with embarrassment."

Desperate for the perfect garden, she tried his advice and proceeded to expose herself to her plants twice daily. Two weeks passed and her neighbor stopped by to check her progress. He asked if she had had any luck with her tomatoes. "No," she replied, "but you should see the size of my cucumbers!!!"

We had a long discussion about how to do this. The goal all along was to have the book be a small version of the website and the mailing list. While we couldn't do the Babes & Hunks, we thought we'd do our best to let me run my mouth whenever I wanted to. For those of you who could not care less about what I have to say (you're the one with your beer and pretzels saying, "dammit, man, just tell me a joke"), well, then you can safely ignore all of my italicized text. For those of you who like to live vicariously through me I have two things to say: (1) you can pay attention to the italicized text and (2) uhhh . . . we need to buy that "life," OK?

A man decided that it was time to teach his son how to say prayers, so he spent a few nights teaching him the basics. After the kid had learned them well enough to say on his own, his father instructed him that after he was done with the prayers each night, he was to choose someone special and ask for God's blessing for that person.

Well, little kids don't always realize that their pets aren't people, so the first night the little boy said his prayers, he ended with, "And God, please bless my puppy." The guy thought that it was pretty cute. However, the next morning the little dog ran out the door and was killed by a car.

That night the little kid asked God to bless his cat when the prayers were finished. And, sure enough, the next morning the cat slipped out, took on the biggest dog in the neighborhood and became breakfast. The father had started to make a connection here, but decided that it was just coincidence.

But when the kid asked God to bless his goldfish, the father couldn't wait for morning so that he could check up on it. As soon as he looked in the bowl, he saw the fish floating upside down at the top.

That night the little kid ended with, "God, please give an extra special blessing to my father."

The father couldn't sleep. He couldn't eat breakfast in the morning. He was afraid to drive to work. He couldn't get any work done because he was petrified. Finally, quitting time came, and he walked home, expecting to drop dead any minute.

When he arrived home, the house was a mess. His wife was lying on the couch still dressed in her robe. The dishes from breakfast were still on the table and the father was furious. He started yelling at his wife, telling her that he had had the worst day of his life and she hadn't even gotten dressed. She looked at him and said, "Shut up! My day was worse. The mailman had a heart attack on our front porch!"

Three blondes are walking through the forest. They come upon some tracks.

The first blonde says, "They're deer tracks."

The second blonde says, "They're bear tracks."

The third blonde says, "They're moose tracks."

Then a train hits them.

A bus stops and two Italian men get on. They seat themselves and engage in animated conversation. The lady sitting behind them ignores their conversation at first, but she listens in horror as one of the men says the following: "Emma come first. Den I come. Two asses, dey come together. I come again. Two asses, dey come together again. I come again and pee twice. Then I come once-a more."

"You foul-mouthed swine," retorted the lady indignantly, "in this country we don't talk about our sex lives in public!"

"Hey, coola down lady," said the man, "Imma just tellun my friend howa to spella Mississippi."

A man walking down the street noticed a small boy trying to reach the doorbell of a house. Even when he jumped up, he couldn't quite reach it. The man decided to help the boy, so he walked up on to the porch, and pushed the doorbell. He looked down at the boy, smiled and asked, "What now?"

The boy answered, "We run like hell!"

One day President Clinton and Hillary were visiting a chicken farm in Arkansas. Soon after their arrival they were taken off on separate tours. When Hillary passed the chicken pens she paused to ask the man in charge if the rooster copulates more than once each day. "Dozens of times," was the reply. "Please tell that to the President," Hillary requested.

When the President passed the pens and was told about the roosters, he asked, "Same hen every time?"

"Oh no, Mr. President, a different one each time."

The President nodded slowly, then said, "Tell that to Mrs. Clinton."

A desperate young mother had two incorrigible boys. Having exhausted all suggestions for controlling the little hellions, she tried one last approach: she took them to the meanest preacher in town for a lecture.

First the older boy was admitted into the stern minister's study.

Glaring at the boy from behind the desk, the preacher waited a few moments, then challenged the boy: "Young man, where is God?"

The boy was stunned to silence.

The preacher rose part way out of his chair and repeated the question: "I asked you, Where Is God?"

The boy began to quake with dread. This was no ordinary lecture for being bad!

Stepping around from behind the desk, the impassioned preacher now shouted his question, "WHERE IS GOD!?"

At this, the boy leaped from his chair and bolted out the door, running headlong into his little brother.

"What's wrong? What's the matter?" his brother asked.

"It's awful! The church has LOST GOD and they're BLAMING US!"

A woman accompanied her husband to the doctor's office. After his checkup, the doctor called the wife into his office alone.

He said: "If you don't do the following, your husband will surely die:

1. Each morning, fix him a healthy breakfast.

2. Be pleasant and make sure he is in a good mood.
3. For lunch, make him a nutritious meal.
4. For dinner, prepare him an especially nice meal.
5. Don't burden him with chores as he probably had a hard day.
6. Don't discuss your problems with him.
7. And most importantly, have sex with him several times a week and satisfy his every whim."

On the way home, the husband asked his wife what the doctor said to her. "You're going to die," she replied.

A girl walks into her parents' bedroom and sees her mother on top of her father. So later that day, she asks her mom what she was doing. Her mom says, "I was bouncing on top of him to try to make him lose some weight." The girl tells her mom, "But Mom, that's not gonna work." The mom thinks, what a smart child. "Why not?" she asks her daughter. The girl replies, "Because every day when you leave, the lady next door comes by and blows him back up."

A young gynecologist was fortunate to have a very beautiful young woman as a patient. One day he was taken with her beauty when she was in the stirrups. Seizing the opportunity he said, "My dear, this next examination could be a little uncomfortable. Shall I numb it for you?" When she consented, he buried his face in her lovely snatch and went, "num num num num num . . ."

This is one of my favorite jokes after I've had four or five beers. It's almost impossible to screw it up and you look like an idiot doing the "num num" line.

The local bar was so sure that its bartender was the strongest man around that it offered a standing $1,000 bet.

The bartender would squeeze a lemon until all the juice ran into a glass, and hand the lemon to a patron. Anyone who could squeeze one more drop of juice out would win the money.

Many people had tried over time (weight lifters, longshoremen, etc.) but nobody could do it.

One day this scrawny little man came in, wearing thick glasses and a polyester suit, and said in a tiny, squeaky voice, "I'd like to try the bet."

After the laughter had died down, the bartender said OK, grabbed a lemon, and squeezed away. Then he handed the wrinkled remains of the rind to the little man.

But the crowd's laughter turned to total silence as the man clenched his fist around the lemon and six drops of juice fell into the glass.

As the crowd cheered, the bartender paid the $1,000, and asked the little man, "What do you do for a living? Are you a lumberjack, a weight lifter, or what?"

The man replied, "I work for the IRS."

It seems that when God was making the world, he called Man over and bestowed upon him twenty years of normal sex life. Man was horrified "Only twenty years of normal sex life?" but the Lord was very adamant -- that was all Man could have.

Then the Lord called the monkey and gave him twenty years. "But I don't need twenty years," he protested, "ten is plenty for me." Man spoke up eagerly, "Can I have the other ten?" The monkey graciously agreed.

Then the Lord called the lion and gave him twenty years, and the lion, like the monkey wanted only ten. Again the Man spoke up, "Can I have the other ten?" The lion said that of course he could.

Then came the donkey and he was given twenty years -- but like the others, ten was sufficient, and again Man pleaded, "Can I have the other ten?"

This explains why man has twenty years of normal sex life, plus ten years of monkeying around, ten years of lion about it and ten years of making an ass of himself.

A young executive was leaving the office at 6 p.m. when he found the CEO standing in front of a shredder with a piece of paper in his hand.

"Listen," said the CEO, "this is a very sensitive and important document, and my secretary has left. Can you make this thing work?"

"Certainly," said the young executive. He turned the machine on, inserted the paper, and pressed the start button.

"Excellent, excellent!" said the CEO as his paper disappeared inside the machine. "I just need one copy."

One day, a father and his son were walking in the woods on their way home when suddenly they came upon two dogs mating in the brush. "What are they doing, Dad?" asked the small child, staring intently at the scene before them.

"They, um, they're making a puppy," said the boy's father, as he grabbed his coat and moved him along quickly. A few nights later, the little boy woke up and got up from his bed to go to the bathroom. As he walked by his parents' room, he heard strange noises coming from within. He opened the door and was surprised to see his father on top of his mother, moving in a strange way. His father looked up and saw his son -- instantly, both mother and father froze. As the boy's mother grabbed for the sheets to cover herself up, the father got up and hustled his son out of the bedroom.

"What were you doing to Mom, Dad?" asked the little boy, who still wasn't sure what he saw.

"Your mother and I were, well, we were, ah, trying to make a baby -- you know, maybe a brother or sister for you," said the boy's father, now confident that this would satisfy his son's curiosity.

"Oh," said the little boy, thinking hard for a minute. "Y'know Dad, when you go back to bed with Mom, turn her over, please -- I'd rather have a puppy."

A guy walks into a bar with an octopus on his shoulder. The bartender says, "You can't bring that in here!"

The guy says, "Why not? He's a pet. Plus I'll bet you a drink he can play any instrument in here."

The bartender says "OK, here's a trombone. I'll bet a drink he can't play it."

The octopus picks it up and starts playing a tune.

The bartender is a little upset and pulls out a clarinet and says, "I bet another drink he can't play this."

The guy says OK and the octopus picks up the clarinet and starts playing away on it.

By now the bartender is really upset. He's had to give the guy 2 free drinks already. Then he remembers he has an old set of bagpipes in the back. He tells the guy, "I'll bet you one more drink he can't play something else I have," and throws out the bagpipes.

The octopus takes one look at the set of bagpipes and starts swarming all over it, pulling on the pipes and squeezing the bag. The bartender laughs and says, "I guess I win."

The guy says, "Just give him a minute. As soon as he realizes he can't fuck it, he'll play it."

A woman is lying on a gurney out in the hall prior to going to surgery. As she lies there, a man in white coat comes by, lifts up the sheet, and then leaves. This happens a second time. The third time this happens she says, "Doctor, am I going into surgery soon?" The man replies, "Don't ask me, Lady. I'm just a painter!"

A little boy gets up to go to the bathroom in the middle of the night. As he passes his parents' bedroom he peeks in through the keyhole. He watches for a moment, then continues on down the hallway, saying to himself, "Boy, and she gets mad at me for sucking my thumb."

This guy decides he's going to play a little joke on his wife one day. As she steps out of the shower, he grabs one of her breasts and says, "If you firmed these up a bit, you wouldn't have to keep using your bra." He laughs and laughs.

The next morning, he again catches her as she finishes her shower and grabs her ass and says, "If you firmed this up a bit, you wouldn't have to keep using your girdle." Again he laughs and laughs, while his wife plots her revenge. The next morning as he steps out of the shower, his wife grabs his penis and says, "If you firmed THIS up a bit, I wouldn't need to keep sleeping with your brother."

A young man took a blind date to an amusement park.

They went for a ride on the Ferris wheel. After the ride, she seemed rather bored.

"What would you like to do next?" he asked.

"I wanna be weighed," she said. So the young man took her over to the weight guesser. "One-twelve," said the man at the scale, and he was absolutely right.

Next they rode the roller coaster. After that, he bought her some popcorn and cotton candy, then he asked what else she would like to do.

"I wanna be weighed," she said.

I really latched onto a square one tonight, thought the young man, and using the excuse that he had developed a headache, he took the girl home.

The girl's mother was surprised to see her home so early, and asked, "What's wrong, dear, didn't you have a nice time tonight?"

"Wousy," said the girl.

A lady awoke one morning and discovered her dog was not moving. She called her vet who asked her to bring the dog in.   After a brief examination, the vet pronounced the dog dead.

"Are you sure?" the distraught woman asked. "He was a great family pet. Isn't there anything else you can do?"

The vet paused for a moment and said, "There is one more thing we can do." He left the room for a moment and came back carrying a large cage with a cat in it. The vet opened the cage door and the cat walked over to the dog. The cat sniffed the dog from head to toe and walked back to the cage.

"Well, that confirms it." the vet announced.   "Your dog is dead." Satisfied that the vet had done everything he possibly could, the woman sighed, "How much do I owe you?"

"That will be $330." the vet replied.

"I don't believe it!!!" screamed the woman. "What did you do that cost $330!?"

"Well," the vet replied, "it's $30 for the office visit and $300 for the cat scan."

So this guy wants to go into a nightclub, but the bouncer says, "Sorry, bud, you need a tie for this place."

Our Hero goes back to his car and rummages around, but there's no necktie to be found. Finally, in desperation, he takes his jumper cables, wraps them around his neck, ties a nice knot, and lets the ends dangle free.

Back to the nightclub, where the bouncer says, "Well, fine, I guess you can come in. But don't start anything."

Two English ladies were discussing their vacation plans on a London street corner near an Irish lady.

"We're planning a lovely holiday in Devon this year," said one.

"Oh, you oughtn't to do that," said the other, "there are Irish there! It would be awful."

"Dear me!" said the first lady. "Well, where are you going?"

"Salisbury," she replied.

"But Salisbury is simply crawling with Irish!" the first objected.

At this point the Irish lady could no longer hold her tongue. "Why don't ye go t' hell," she suggested. "There be no Irish there!"

A very small, sickly-looking man was hired as a bartender. The saloon owner gave him a word of warning, "Drop everything and run for your life if ever you hear that 'Big John' is on his way to town." The man worked several months without any problems.

Then one day a cowhand rushed in shouting, "Big John is a'comin'," and knocked the small bartender on the floor in his hurry to get out.

Before the bartender had a chance to recover, a giant of a man with a black bushy beard rode into the saloon, on the back of a buffalo, using a rattlesnake for a whip, through the swinging doors. The man tore the doors off their hinges, knocked over tables, and flung the snake into the corner. He then took his massive fist and split the bar in half as he asked for a drink. The bartender nervously pushed a bottle at the man. He bit off the top of the bottle with his teeth and downed the contents in one gulp, and turned to leave. Seeing that he wasn't hurting anyone, the bartender asked the man if he would like another drink.

"I ain't got no time," the man roared. "Big John is a'comin' to town."

"AOL subscribers pay your salary!"

CIG from AOL

okay you think you are a big genius. just remember. AOL subscribers pay your salary. call me anything you like. you are sadistic!!!!

if you have seen all my messages, surely you can tell me what the problem is.

maybe you don't know. is it the parenthesis, capitals in the address, wrong address sent to. I think you have tortured me enough. call me anything. just get me off this damned list.

Jeeezus . . .

AOL subscribers do NOT pay my salary, bonehead.

Yes, I can tell you what your problem is: you're an idiot.

Susie with AOL

not all of us aol users are dum.

Donna with Juno

Dearest Ray,

I have watched your comments over the last couple of months, and have been enchanted. Will you marry me?

Love, Donna

Shell with carroll.com
Wow. Remind me **never** to get in a flame war with you. You are a flame God.

Your wit and intelligence continuous to amaze me!

Your jokes make a stressful day at work much easier to deal with. For that, I thank you.

Oh and . . .

If you and Donna get married, (see previous message), can I be your mistress? ;-)

Mindy from Juno
hello... do i have to email you a thousand times??? DELETE MY ACCOUNT

Hello, do you have to be told a MILLION times -- learn how to read, idiot. When you figure out the unsubscribe instructions, THEN you can get off the list. And not ONE second before.

Excuse me but my daughter and I have never been so insulted in our lives. That is hardly the type of email you should be writing to a 13yr old girl who was trying to erase herself from your mailing list. I will have you know that I am a columnist for a major magazine and I will definetly be writing an upcoming column about a poorly run internet circulation known as "Jokeaday." It will be every intention of mine to persuade people against signing up and persuade people even further from advertising on your site. Thank you for your time, if I can convince just a few people, based on your rudeness towards customers to stop subscribing to you, then I have accomplished something. Haven't you ever heard the term "the customer is always right." Well I hope you don' t miss my column about you, I will be emailing you a copy in the near future... until then, goodbye!

Well, Mindy, then you should learn how to police what your daughter is doing on the Internet. Sounds to me as if your parenting skills need some work.

Now, let's get a couple of ground rules down before you go mouthing off without all of the facts. If you **do** *write for a major magazine, then surely you'll want to have the "facts" straight. Then again, with the media the way they are, the "facts" more than likely don't concern you.*

If your "13-year-old" was smart enough to figure out how to get ON the list, then she should be smart enough to figure out how to get OFF the list. There are unsubscribe instructions plastered on EVERY item we send out. There are unsubscribe instructions on the www page. There are FAQ and Help documents that are mentioned in EVERY thing we send out.

In addition, your "13-year-old" also received a welcome letter, which stated in NO UNCERTAIN TERMS that she was NOT welcome here. People under 18 have NO business here. She was told to IMMEDIATELY unsubscribe and HOW to unsubscribe. She obviously ignored THOSE warnings, too.

In short, this "13-year-old" is being taught valuable lessons by two sources: **I'm** *teaching her how to take responsibility for her actions -- i.e., unsubscribe from a listing that she had no business on in the first place.* **You** *are teaching her that there IS no responsibility for her actions, that she can ignore warnings, ignore instructions, and ignore how things work and life will be grand. Man, I'm glad I didn't have parents like YOU.*

This "13-year-old" is NOT my customer -- no more than if I owned a liquor store or gun shop or ran a movie theater that plays "R" rated movies -- she's not WELCOME here. She had no BUSINESS here. She KNEW that but now has decided to complain about it. Funny -- she breaks the rules willingly but it's someone else's fault.

Do be sure to write THAT in your "major magazine," Mindy. That is, **if** *you're interested in the facts of an article.*

I can assure you that my daughter did not recieve any such notice about being too young to be a subscriber to the jokeaday newsletter. I am sure of this because as a concerned parent, and having written articles about internet meetings ending in rape and such thing, I read all of her email that she recieves. All I am trying to point out to you is that you have no business speaking in such terms to anyone like that. All youwould have to simply say is email such and such address and your account will be removed. How difficult is that? Thank you sir for you time, however, you still have not convinced me that Jokeaday is worth being spared embaressment in my upcoming publication.

Then you're way out of the loop. And your reading and writing skills are obviously comparable to your daughter's.

*If you REALLY read **any** of the mails that were sent to her address for her subscription, then you would notice at the TOP (that's called the masthead, by the way) of EVERY document sent out are the unsubscribe instructions. If you have a Juno account, Juno is quite capable of recognizing a mailto: hyperlink. All she'd have to do is click on the hyperlink to create a unique message that would definitely unsubscribe her. No muss, no fuss -- and completely idiot proof ONLY if you know how to read and follow directions. You say, "all I [had] to do was simply say such &such." Why? It's in everything that goes out. Why are you and your daughter deserving of "special treatment" and/or special instructions/handling?*

Now, if you CAN'T read and follow directions -- well, isn't that the classic definition of an idiot? And if you're an idiot, then, by all means, that should be pointed out to you. I don't have the time or inclination to coddle people who get on the Internet, sign up for my subscription, use my computer resources, and complain about it. Your daughter has cost me money in time and computer resources. People like that infuriate me. If you are encouraging this kind of behavior, then YOU are an idiot, also.

Your daughter could not have possibly been on this listing WITHOUT having received a confirmation letter AND a welcome letter. That's the way it works here, Mindy. You can tell me until you're blue in the face that you "didn't get one." I run this organization and I know EXACTLY how it works. If you didn't get the confirmation letter and/or the welcome letter, then you wouldn't get the subscription, either. It's just that simple.

*Believe me when I tell you that the last thing on my mind was "pleading" with you to "spare" me your wrath in your upcoming publication, Mindy. I couldn't care less **what** you write because from here all you've demonstrated is that you'll bend the "facts" to spare you and your daughter. Hey, I've got kids and I understand wanting to believe and protect them. But never would I relieve my child of her obligation to follow through on her responsibilities -- no matter how many excuses I can make for her. My side of the story will be waiting for your readers on **my** site. I'll enjoy the publicity.*

Besides, how serious could anyone take an article of yours when you spell it "embaressment"?

"Our supermarket had a sale on boneless chicken breasts . . . "

Our supermarket had a sale on boneless chicken breasts, and a woman I know intended to stock up. At the store, however, she was disappointed to find only a few skimpy prepackaged portions of the poultry, so she complained to the butcher. "Don't worry, lady," he said. "I'll pack some more trays and have them ready for you by the time you finish shopping."

Several aisles later, my friend heard the butcher's voice boom over the public-address system: "Will the lady who wanted bigger breasts please meet me at the back of the store?"

A hippie gets onto a bus and proceeds to sit next to a nun in the front seat. The hippie looks over and asks the nun if she would have sex with him.

The nun, surprised by the question, politely declines and gets off at the next stop. When the bus starts on its way the bus driver says to the hippie, "If you want, I can tell you how you can get that nun to have sex with you."

The hippie, of course, says that he'd love to know, so the bus driver tells him that every Tuesday evening at midnight the nun goes to the cemetery to pray to the Lord. "If you went dressed in robes and some glowing powder," said the bus driver guy, "you could tell her you were God and command her to have sex with you."

Well, the hippie decides to try this out. That Tuesday he goes to the cemetery and waits for the nun. Right on schedule the nun shows up. When she's in the middle of praying, the hippie walks out from hiding, in robes and glowing with a mask of God. "I am God, I have heard your prayers and will answer them, but you must have sex with me first."

The nun agrees but asks for anal sex so she might keep her virginity. The hippie agrees to this and quickly sets about to go to work on the nun.

After the hippie finishes, he rips off his mask and shouts out, "Ha ha, I'm the hippie!!"

The nun replies by whipping off her mask and shouts, "Ha ha, I'm the bus driver!!"

Scientists were preparing an experiment to ask the ultimate question. They had worked for months gathering one each of every computer that had ever been built. Finally the big day was at hand. All the computers were linked together. They asked the question, "IS THERE A GOD?"

Suddenly there was a loud crash, and in a brilliant explosion of silicon and plastic the computers fused into what appeared to the scientists to be one large computer in place of the many smaller ones. One of the scientists raced to the printer as it finally output its answer.

"There is now," read the printout.

Two smart, attractive, well-educated young law graduates, Sally and Edith, were competing for a prestigious job. As part of the job interview each was asked why she wanted the job. Edith answered that she wanted to work for a firm with a reputation of being concerned with truth and justice. When it was her turn, Sally simply opened her purse, took out a rather thin wallet and laid it on the senior partner's desk. "I want to fatten it up as fast as possible," she said.

Sally got the job.

A man is passing a butcher's shop and sees a sign:

Special Offer -- Brains

Cow brains	$1 a pound
Sheep brains	$2 a pound
Pig brains	$2 a pound
Doctor brains	$50 a pound
Engineer brains	$50 a pound
Programmer brains	$50 a pound
Lawyer brains	$1000 a pound

He goes into the shop and says to the butcher, "Excuse me, I couldn't help noticing your sign -- I suppose the cow brains are so much cheaper than the other brains because cows are so common."

"That's right," says the butcher.

"And," continues the man, "I suppose the lawyer brains are so much more expensive than the other brains because they're such high quality."

"Not at all," says the butcher "do you know how many lawyers you gotta kill to get a pound of brain?"

At one time in 1998 I had four lawyers on my payroll. Damned vultures, every one of 'em. In 1999 things got worse. Now there are five of 'em. Personally, I'm with Bill Shakespeare on the whole "Lawyer Reduction Act" -- kill 'em all.

A farmer in Arkansas and his wife were lying in bed one evening; she was knitting, he was reading the latest issue of *Animal Husbandry*. He looks up from the page and says to her, "Did you know that humans are the only species in which the female achieves orgasm?"

She looks at him wistfully, smiles, and replies, "Oh yeah? Prove it."

He frowns for a moment, then says, "OK." He then gets up and walks out, leaving his wife with a confused look on her face.

About half an hour later he returns all tired and sweaty and says, "Well, I'm sure the cow and sheep didn't, but the way that pig squealed, it's hard to tell."

A woman walks into a bar and orders two shots. She downs the first one. "This is for the shame," and then the second one, "This is for the glory."

She then orders two more shots. She drinks the first one. "This is for the shame" and then the second one, "this is for the glory."

She is about to order two more shots when the bartender stops her. "Ma'am, I was just wondering: what's this about shame and glory?"

"Well," she replies, "I like to do my housework naked. But when I bent over to pick something up, my Great Dane mounted me from behind."

"That must be the shame," the bartender said.

"No, that was the glory. The shame is when we got locked up and he dragged me around the front yard for thirty minutes."

One of my first evenings back from overseas, my girl's understanding parents left us alone in the living room.

Naturally, we did not talk all the time. In the midst of a kiss, I noticed her little sister in her nightgown watching us from the doorway.

"If you will be a good girl and go to bed, I will give you a quarter," I said to her.

Without taking the bribe or saying a word, she ran off but soon was back again.

"Here is a dollar," she said. "I wanna watch."

"Look, Solomon, I'm not one to complain, but don't you think you're a little greedy having a thousand wives? I mean, what can you do with a thousand wives that you can't do with just one?"

"Oh, I do the same thing, but the odds of them all having a headache are a lot less!"

A kindergartner was practicing spelling with magnetic letters on the refrigerator: cat, dog, dad, and mom had been proudly displayed for all to see.

One morning while getting ready for the day, he bounded into the room with his arms outstretched. In his hands were three magnetic letters: G-O-D.

"Look what I spelled, Mom!" with a proud smile on his face.

"That's wonderful!" his mom praised him. "Now go put them on the fridge so Dad can see when he gets home tonight."

The mom happily thought that her son's Catholic education was certainly having an impact.

Just then, a little voice called from the kitchen: "Mom? How do you spell 'zilla'?"

A very successful businessman had a meeting with his new son-in-law. "I love my daughter, and now I welcome you into the family," said the man. "To show you how much we care for you, I'm making you a 50-50 partner in my business. All you have to do is go to the factory every day and learn the operations."

The son-in-law interrupted. "I hate factories. I can't stand the noise."

"I see," replied the father-in-law. "Well, then, you'll work in the office and take charge of some of the operations."

"I hate office work," said the son-in-law. "I can't stand being stuck behind a desk all day."

"Wait a minute," said the father-in-law. "I make you half-owner of a moneymaking organization, but you don't like factories and won't work in an office. What am I going to do with you?"

"Easy," said the young man. "Buy me out."

A lawyer was well into a lengthy cross-examination of a witness, when he stopped and said, "Your honor, a juror is asleep."

The judge ruled: "You put him to sleep; YOU wake him up."

The Zen Master from Tibet is visiting New York City. He goes up to a hot dog vendor and says, "Make me one with everything."

The hot dog vendor fixes a hot dog and hands it to the Zen Master, who pays with a $20 bill.

The vendor puts the bill in the cash box and closes it. "Where's my change?" asks the Zen Master.

The vendor responds, "Change must come from within."

I love puns. When I was about 6 my mom stuck me in the closet and told me I couldn't come out until I'd made a pun. I said, "OK, O-Pun the door." Nyuk nyuk.

A couple was celebrating their golden wedding anniversary. Their domestic tranquillity had long been the talk of the town. A local newspaper reporter was inquiring as to the secret of their long and happy marriage.

"Well, it dates back to our honeymoon," explained the lady. "We visited the Grand Canyon and took a trip down to the bottom of the canyon by pack mule. We hadn't gone too far when my husband's mule stumbled."

"My husband quietly said, 'That's once.' We proceeded a little farther when the mule stumbled again. Once more my husband quietly said, 'That's twice.' We hadn't gone a half-mile when the mule stumbled a third time. My husband took a pistol from his pocket and shot him."

"I started to protest over his treatment of the mule when he looked at me and quietly said, 'That's once.'"

*You would not believe the mail I got after I ran this joke.   Animal Rights activists came out of the woodwork flinging knives and other cutlery. Now, go figure, I tell a joke where some **person** gets blown to hell and I won't hear a peep. But you let me harm a (pay attention here, PETA) fictional animal, they go wild.*

Reminds me of the article that The Onion *did after the* Challenger *blew up. They said, in addition to the 7 astronauts aboard, there were also cute duckies, baby seals, fuzzy kittens, and orphans. Most of the folks didn't give a shit about the orphans, but "oh, those poor little baby seals!"*

Mrs. Grednik, who was a little on the chubby side, was at her Weight Watchers meeting. "My husband insists I come to these meetings because he would rather screw a woman with a trim figure," she lamented to the woman next to her.

"Well," the lady replied, "what's wrong with that?"

"He likes to do it while I'm stuck at these damn meetings."

A woman was waiting in the checkout line at a shopping center. Her arms were heavily laden with a mop and broom and other cleaning supplies. By her actions and deep sighs, it was obvious she was in a hurry and not happy about the slowness of the line.

When the cashier called for a price check on a box of soap, the woman remarked indignantly, "Well, I'll be lucky to get out of here and home before Christmas!"

"Don't worry, ma'am," replied the clerk. "With that wind kicking up out there and that brand new broom you have here, you'll be home in no time."

Speaking at the staff meeting, a very pert and pretty female engineer named Rene told the male manager of the division, "I'd like to get something off my chest."

"What's that, Rene?"

"Your eyes."

A preacher was completing a temperance sermon, when, with great expression, he said, "If I had all the beer in the world, I'd take it and throw it into the river."

With even greater emphasis he said, "And if I had all the wine in the world, I'd take it and throw it into the river."

And then finally, he said, "And if I had all the whiskey in the world, I'd take it and throw it into the river." He sat down.

The song leader then stood very cautiously and announced with a smile, "For our closing song, let us sing Hymn 365: "Shall We Gather at the River."

A professor of chemistry wanted to teach his 5th grade class a lesson about the evils of liquor, so he produced an experiment that involved a glass of water, a glass of whiskey, and two worms.

"Now, class. Observe closely the worms," said the professor putting a worm first into the water. The worm in the water wiggled about, happy as a worm in water could be.

The second worm he put into the whiskey. It writhed painfully, and quickly sank to the bottom, dead as a doornail.

"Now, what lesson can we derive from this experiment?" the professor asked.

Johnny, who naturally sits in back, raised his hand and wisely responded, "Drink whiskey and you won't get worms."

Jon was driving when a policeman pulled him over. He rolled down his window and said to the officer, "Is there a problem, Officer?"

"No problem at all. I just observed your safe driving and am pleased to award you a $5,000 Safe Driver Award. Congratulations. What do you think you're going to do with the money?"

Jon thought for a minute and said, "Well, I guess I'll go get that drivers' license."

Judi, sitting in the passenger seat, said to the policeman, "Oh, don't pay attention to him -- he's a smartass when he's drunk and stoned."

Brian from the backseat said, "I TOLD you guys we wouldn't get far in a stolen car!!!"

At that moment, there was a knock from the trunk and Amanpreet's muffled voice said, "Are we over the border yet?"

At the beginning of a children's sermon, one girl came up to the altar wearing a beautiful dress. As the children were sitting down around the pastor, the pastor leans over and says to the girl, "That is a very pretty dress. Is it your Easter dress?"

The girl replied almost directly into the pastor's clip-on mike, "Yes. And my mom says it's a bitch to iron."

For the first time in many years, an old man traveled from his rural town to the city to attend a movie. After buying his ticket, he stopped at the concession stand to purchase some popcorn. Handing the attendant $1.50, he couldn't help but comment, "The last time I came to the movies, popcorn was only 15 cents."

"Well, sir," the attendant replied with a grin, "You're really going to enjoy yourself. We have sound now."

"No, it's not the 'pickle joke.'"

Jenn in Sacramento

Ray, I love your site, really I do, but I gotta let you know I am disappointed in you today.

No, it's not the pickle joke (*see the section in the back of this book about the Jokes That Launched The Judi Awards*), and it's not Ghandi or God, and I am pretty sure that I could figure out how the heck to unsub if I wanted to. It's the 'Nad Award, Ray. I finally got the chance to check it out this evening, and I must say I was very disappointed. Your Babes all have nice-sized jugs because that is what red-blooded American guys like Mr. Jokeaday like (fortunately for the women in my family). I can understand that even though I belong to the other gender (the one with the jugs), and it's okay with me. Men should be like that, you know? We like that in a guy, trust me.

But your 'Nad award? It's a size thing, Ray. It's just not much to look at, if you know what I mean. No offense to the guy who posed for it or anything, but...there's gotta be a more to life than that!

I have an idea! Couldn't YOU pose for a more 'fulfilling' 'Nad Award? I can't think of anyone better! I know the award is designed to make cruel (but well deserved) fun of idiots, but at least if it is, well, more impressive, perhaps it'll make an even 'bigger' impression on the morons to whom it is dedicated. After all, they'll never be on either the giving or the receiving (depending on their preference) end of such a set of truly gifted organs, so you may as well really stick it to them (figuratively speaking, of course) with a new, improved 'Nad Award.

I guess what I am trying to say is, if you are going to hang male genitalia in our faces in the name of humor, at least make it worth our while, okay?

Thanks for listening, I feel better to have shared my concerns with you. It is comforting to know that you always have your subscribers' best interests close to your heart and that you always treat us with dignity and respect (except when we're stupid, of course)!

With anticipation and no stupid e-mail abbreviations,

Jenn in rainy Sacramento

(Although on the topic of 'nads, you might appreciate the name of my brother's softball team--The 'Nads. That way the people in the stands could yell "Go Nads!" Gotta love that.)

Hi Jenn:

You know, I actually thought about it. I scoured the 'net looking for clinical pictures of 'nads, but couldn't find anything. Then I realized -- hell, go out to a gay site. There's 'nads galore out there.

I found a bunch of 'em. But then I realized I'd probably run afoul of pornography laws if I displayed those 'nads. (Yeah, I know, it's a double standard -- tits you can show, 'nads you can't.)

And yes, I do know 'bout the 'Nads. In fact, that was the first site I went to -- just to see :)

*Finally, if I hung **my** nads out there, the sheer size of them would make other men hang their heads in despair and shame. Women would swoon and file for divorce/leave boyfriends en masse because "there's something much better out there." There'd be rioting in the streets, congressional inquiries, TIME Magazine would make me Man of the Century, and the Y2K end of civilization would look puny in comparison. So, in the interest of saving the world (isn't that my self-appointed task every day?) I guess I better keep 'em zipped up and bring 'em out only for special State Ceremonies.*

Ray
Joke A Day

Ray, that's what I so admire about you--your utter selfless dedication to the betterment of mankind (I suppose even a simple line drawing would just be too much for this world to handle, wouldn't it?!) It brings a tear to my eye and a lump to my throat. Where's the Kleenex?

Kris with AOL
I'm a big fan of joke a day and have been for quite some time, but the January 7th joke about the Pope telling the bum to "get the hell out of here" was really quite offensive. I personally enjoy offensive jokes, especially when they're told by an equal opportunity offender such as yourself, but telling a joke like that about a person who does so much good and is deserving of every person's admiration and respect is wrong in my eyes and I ask that you please refrain from doing so in the future.

Why does he deserve my admiration? I'm not Catholic and have no beliefs that this guy is anything but a plain old human being -- no more special than you or me, Kris.

Orval with swbell
Even though I am a retired minister, I think the Jesus - Paul joke is hilarious. You need to make an adjustment before filing it in your archives. Paul was not there - he did not come along until many years later and says, himself, that he never saw Jesus in the flesh, only in a vision, on the road to Damascus. You could use one of the 12 disciples: Peter, Andrew, James, John, Thaddeus, Bartholomew, Thomas, Jude (James the Less), Matthew, Philip, or Simon (see Mark 3:14-19), but not Judas, who had committed suicide by now.

Keep up the good work. Do not worry about people who get offended. They are not your judges. Just lay off the President - he has enough critics.

Now, Pastor, you were doing fine until you got to the Clinton stuff. :)

On the other hand, when I was home this Christmas, my own mother admitted she voted for him. I'm thinking about having auditions for another mom.

Take care and glad to have you with me, sir!

Ray
Joke A Day

"So, let me get this straight . . ."

"So, let me get this straight," the prosecutor says to the defendant, "you came home from work early and found your wife in bed with a strange man."

"That's correct," says the defendant.

"Upon which," continues the prosecutor, "you take out a pistol and shoot your wife, killing her."

"That's correct," says the defendant.

"Then my question to you is, why did you shoot your wife and not her lover?" asked the prosecutor.

"It seemed easier," replied the defendant, "than shooting a different man every day!"

A foursome is waiting at the men's tee while another foursome of ladies is hitting from the ladies' tee.

The ladies are taking their time, and when finally the last one is ready to hit the ball, she hacks it about 10 feet, goes over to it and hacks it another 10 feet, looks up at the men who are watching, and says apologetically: "I guess all those fucking lessons I took this winter didn't help."

One of the men immediately replies, "No, you see that's your problem. You should have taken 'golf' lessons instead."

In a crowded airliner, a five-year-old boy is throwing a wild temper tantrum. No matter what his frustrated, embarrassed mother does to try to calm him down, the boy continues to scream furiously and kick the seats around him.

Suddenly, from the rear of the plane, an elderly minister slowly walks forward up the aisle. Stopping the flustered mother with an upraised hand, the kindly, white-haired, soft-spoken minister leans down and whispers something into the boy's ear.

Instantly, the boy calms down, gently takes his mother's hand, and quietly fastens his seat belt.

All the other passengers burst into spontaneous applause. As the minister slowly makes his way back to his seat, one of the stewardesses takes him by the sleeve.

"Excuse me, Reverend," she says quietly, "but what magic words did you use on that little boy?"

The old man smiles serenely and gently says, "I told him if he didn't cut that shit out, I'd kick his frikkin' ass to the moon."

A guy took a girl out on her first date. When they pulled off into a secluded area around midnight, the girl said, "My mother told me to say no to everything."

"Well," he said, "do you mind if I put my arm around you?"

"Uhhh . . . no," the girl replied.

"Do you mind if I put my other hand on your leg?"

"N-n-no," the girl stammered.

"You know," he said, "We're going to have a lot of fun if you're on the level about this."

Jesus saw a crowd chasing down a woman to stone her and approached them. "What's going on here, anyway?" he asked.

"This woman was found committing adultery and the law says we should stone her!" one of the crowd responded.

"Wait," yelled Jesus, "Let he who is without sin cast the first stone."

Suddenly, a stone was thrown from out of the sky, and knocked the woman on the side of her head.

"Aw, c'mon, Dad," Jesus cried, "I'm trying to make a point here!"

A businessman on his deathbed called his friend and said, "Bill, I want you to promise me that when I die you will have my remains cremated."

"And what," his friend asked, "do you want me to do with your ashes?"

The businessman said, "Just put them in an envelope and mail them to the Internal Revenue Service and write on the envelope, 'Now you have everything.'"

A guy was playing golf at some fancy club, and just as he was about to tee off, a cart drives up. These two guys get out and hand him a note saying, "We are deaf; may we play through?"

The guy says, "Hell no!" and tees off anyway.

Later on (after six shots), he is on the green about to putt when a ball comes from out of nowhere and misses his head by an inch. "What the @#$%^&*?" he yells.

The deaf guys drive up and hand him a note. On the note is written, "FORE."

An elderly patient needed a heart transplant and discussed his options with his doctor. The doctor said, "We have three possible donors; the first is a young, healthy athlete who died in an automobile accident, the second is a middle-aged businessman who never drank or smoked and who died flying his private jet. The third is an attorney who died after practicing law for 30 years. Which do you want?"

"I'll take the lawyer's heart," said the patient.

After a successful transplant, the doctor asked the patient why he had chosen the donor he did. "It was easy," said the patient, "I wanted a heart that hadn't been used."

A married couple was enjoying a dinner out when a statuesque blonde walked over to their table, exchanged warm greetings with the husband, and walked off.

"Who was that?" the wife demanded.

"If you must know," the husband replied, "that was my mistress."

"Your mistress? That's it! I want a divorce!" the wife fumed.

The husband looked her straight in the eye and said, "Are you sure you want to give up our big house in the suburbs, your Mercedes, your furs, your jewelry, and our vacation home in Mexico?"

For a long time they continued dining in silence. Finally, the woman nudged her husband and said, "Isn't that Howard over there? Who's he with?"

"That's HIS mistress," her husband replied.

"Oh," she said, taking a bite of dessert. "Ours is much cuter."

After being with his blind date all evening, the man couldn't take another minute with her. Earlier, he had secretly arranged to have a friend call him to the phone so he would have an excuse to leave if something like this happened.

When he returned to the table, he lowered his eyes, put on a grim expression and said, "I have some bad news. My grandfather just died."

"Thank heavens," his date replied. "If yours hadn't, mine would have had to!"

Junior was one of those holy terrors and when his mother suggested that they buy him a bike for his birthday, her husband was surprised.

"Do you really believe that'll help improve his behavior?" he said.

"Well, no," she admitted, "But it'll spread it over a wider area."

The newlyweds were suffering from exhaustion and after an examination, their doctor advised, "It's not unusual for young people to overdo things during the first weeks of marriage. What you both need is rest. For the next month I want you to limit your sex life to those days of the week with an 'R' in them. That is, Thursday, Friday and Saturday."

Since the end of the week was approaching the newlyweds had no immediate difficulty following the medico's orders. But on the first night of scheduled rest the young bride found herself eager as a beaver.

Hubby fell asleep, but she tossed and turned and finally nudged her spouse into partial wakefulness.

Expecting daylight, and confused with the darkness, he asked, "What day is it, Honey?"

She looks at him with a gleam in her eyes and says, "Mondray."

Amanpreet had heard a family rumor that his father, grandfather and even his great-grandfather all "walked on water" on their 21st birthday.

So, on his 21st birthday, he and his good friend Brian headed out to the lake. "If they could do it, so can I!" Amanpreet (which means "Lizard Pecker" in several languages) told Brian (which means "Amanpreet" in several languages).

Amanpreet and Brian arrived at the lake and rented a boat. They paddled out to the middle. Amanpreet stepped off the side of the boat . . . and damn near drowned.

Furious, he had Brian drive him back to the Lizard Pecker Family Farm and asked his grandmother why he hadn't been blessed with the same "gift" as the others in the family.

Grandmother Pecker took Amanpreet by the hands, looked into his face, and said, "That's because your father, grandfather, and great-grandfather were born in January. You were born in July."

"Amanpreet" was a gent who wrote in and couldn't figure out the unsubscribe instructions, either. (Ahh, so many boneheads, so little time.) He wound up winning a "Judi Award" for his follow up letters, and I wound up telling him that his name means "Lizard Pecker" in several languages.

I reuse all of the "Judi Award" winners names in jokes. I'm particularly fond of "Amanpreet" because . . . well . . . it sounds so stupid.

But every time I use it, I can count on an extra 20 letters each for a few days telling me that I'm being disrespectful to Muslims everywhere by using the name.

Usually I tell 'em that 'Preet was a fat Roman Catholic Irish red-headed guy who changed his name to "Amanpreet" because he thought he'd get less abuse than his birth name: "Lizard Pecker."

One day a young Texas couple decides to get married. After the wedding they leave for their honeymoon. While driving down the road, the new bride sees two cows having sex.

The new bride asks, "What are they doing, Honey?" The husband answers, "They're roping!"

She replies, "Oh, I see!"

After a few more hours of driving they pass two horses having sex. Again the bride asks, "What are they doing, Honey?"

The husband answers, "They're roping!"

She replies, "OK, now I see!"

Finally they arrive at their hotel. The couple wash up and start to get ready for bed. When they get in the bed, they start to explore each other's body. The bride discovers her husband's dick.

"What is that?" she asks.

"That is my rope," he answers.

She slides her hands down further and gasps, "What are those?"

"They are my knots," he answers.

Finally the couple begin to make love. After several minutes the bride says, "Stop, Honey, wait a minute!"

Her husband asks, "What's the matter, Honey?"

The bride replies, "Undo those knots and give me more rope!"

Shakey went to a psychiatrist. "Doc," he said, "I've got trouble. Every time I get into bed, I think there's somebody under it. I get under the bed, I think there's somebody on top of it. Top, under, top, under. You gotta help me, I'm going crazy!"

"Just put yourself in my hands for two years," said the shrink. "Come to me three times a week, and I'll cure your fears."

"How much do you charge?"

"A hundred dollars per visit."

"I'll sleep on it," said Shakey.

Six months later the doctor met Shakey on the street. "Why didn't you ever come to see me again?" asked the psychiatrist.

"For a hundred bucks a visit? A bartender cured me for ten dollars."

"Is that so! How?"

"He told me to cut the legs off the bed!"

Heard on a public transportation vehicle while in Orlando. "When you exit this vehicle, please be sure to lower your head and watch your step.

"If you fail to do so, please lower your voice and watch your language. Thank you."

A completely inebriated man walked into a bar and, after staring for some time at the only woman seated at the bar, walked over to her, placed his hand up her skirt and began fondling her.

She jumped up and slapped him silly.

He immediately apologized and explained, "I'm sorry. I thought you were my wife. You look exactly like her."

"Why you drunken, worthless, insufferable asshole!" she screamed.

"Funny," he muttered, "you even sound exactly like her."

A lawyer cross-examined the adversary's main witness. "You claim to have stopped by Mrs. Edwards' house just after breakfast. Will you tell the jury what she said?"

"Objection, Your Honor," shouted the other lawyer.

There then followed a long argument between the lawyers as to whether the question was proper. Finally, after 45 minutes, the judge allowed it.

"So," the first lawyer continued, "Please answer the question: What did Mrs. Edwards say when you went to her house after breakfast on December 3rd?"

"Nothing," said the witness. "No one was home."

A city boy was visiting the country and wanted to go hunting. The farmer lent the boy his gun, telling him not to kill any farm animals.

The city boy headed off and soon after saw a goat. He managed to creep into range and finally shot it. Not knowing anything about animals, the boy didn't know what he'd killed so he ran to the farmhouse and described his kill to the farmer.

"It had two saggy tits, a beard, a hard head and it stunk like hell!" said the boy.

"Oh, shit!" said the farmer. "You've shot the wife!"

A young boy and his doting grandmother were walking along the seashore when a huge wave appeared out of nowhere, sweeping the child out to sea.

The horrified woman fell to her knees, raised her eyes to the heavens and begged the Lord to return her beloved grandson.

Lo, another wave reared up and deposited the stunned child on the sand before her.

The grandmother looked the boy over carefully. He was fine.

But still she stared up angrily toward the heavens. "When we came," she snapped indignantly, "he had a hat!"

*Stop reading and think about this for a minute: you **know** someone just like this, don't you?*

A guy enters a restaurant, and orders a milkshake,

"Not too thick, not too thin, but in the groove, man, in the groove!"

The cook hears this and gets pissed off, but just sends him the milkshake without saying anything.

The guy then orders a box of fries, "Not too crisp, not too soft, but in the groove, man, in the groove!"

The cook is getting really pissed off at this, but he rolls up his sleeves and gets him the box of fries.

Then the guy orders a hamburger, "Not too big, not too small, but in the groove, man, in the groove."

On hearing this, the cook storms out and charges up to the guy, "You can just kiss my ass!! Not too much to the left, not too much to the right, but in the groove, man, in the groove!"

"My god! What happened to you?" the bartender asked Kelly as he hobbled in on a crutch, one arm in a cast.

"I got in a tiff with Riley."

"Riley? He's just a wee fellow," the barkeep said, surprised. "He must have had something in his hand."

"That he did," Kelly said. "A shovel it was."

"Dear Lord. Didn't you have anything in your hand?"

"Aye, that I did -- Mrs. Riley's tit." Kelly said. "And a beautiful thing it was, but not much use in a fight."

"You seem to have more than the average share of intelligence for a man of your background," sneered the lawyer at a witness on the stand.

"If I wasn't under oath, I'd return the compliment," replied the witness.

Three cowboys are sitting around a campfire, out on the lonesome prairie, each with the bravado for which cowboys are famous. A night of tall tales begins.

The first says, "I must be the meanest, toughest cowboy there is. Why, just the other day, a bull got loose in the corral and gored six men before I wrestled it to the ground, by the horns, with my bare hands."

The second can't stand to be bested. "Why that's nothing. I was walking down the trail yesterday and a fifteen-foot rattler slid out from under a rock and made a move for me. I grabbed that snake with my bare hands, bit its head off, and sucked the poison down in one gulp. And I'm still here today."

The third cowboy remained silent, slowly stirring the coals with his penis.

(to be read in your best scottish accent!)

Two young girls had gone to Scotland for a vacation. While touring they saw a villager in his "kilt". Curious as to what they actually wear under their kilts, one of the girls proceeded to ask the man.

"Excuse me sir, what exactly do men wear under their kilts?" asked the girl.

"Well," replied the man, "reach up there and find out".

The girl pondered his suggestion and then followed it. She reached under his kilt and got a hand full. She exclaimed, "Oh, how gruesome!"

"Why, yes," replied the man in his deep accent, "and if you put your hand up there again it will grew some more."

"Take me off your list if you don't I will involve other people."

Kate415 with AOL
Take me off your list if you don't I will involve other people.

And do what? All of you go join WebTV?

Clayton with cableregina
Just outta curiousity ... if I were to get a friend or 10 to subscribe to 'JAD' do I get any special bonus outta the deal?? :)

Yeah.

You don't have to forward the jokes to ten people anymore. I'll do it for you.

Charlie with Hotmail
I'm a meteorologist and I had to laugh when I saw where you watched the weather channel all week. I watch it some, but not all the time! (Unless there's nothing else to watch)

It's Kristina Abernathy that does it for me. :)

There's Jill Brown and some new girl named Heather Tesh. I mean, there's only so much "high, lows, and isobars" one man can take.

I noticed Jill Brown recently defected to CNN and I was gratified to find her on-camera recently. Life is good.

Esaimson with AOL

I'm glad to see your enjoying all the revenue producing advertising us poor working slobs support while you sit around watching the weather channel for a week!

ES:

*When's the **last** time you:*

*(1) **paid** for a Deluxe Subscription? (2) **paid** for a Babe Subscription? (3) **visited** a sponsor's site? (4) **joined** a sponsor's newsletter? (5) **bought** something from a sponsor's site? (6) **placed** an ad with Joke A Day?*

*If you've not done **any** of these things, you're not supporting me. Support doesn't require that you actually **purchase** something -- but if you're not doing one of the six things above, then you're NOT supporting Joke A Day.*

This sounds like a classic case of jealousy and envy on your part, ES. What you see is me sitting around, watching TV, telling jokes, looking at babe pictures, and sending out a couple of emails every day. Easy money, huh?

*What you **don't** see is the 70+ hours a week, the constant drive to acquire advertising revenue (so people, like you, don't have to PAY for this service), the endless email requiring answers, technical questions to be answered on a daily basis, the constant revisions to the documentation and web site (the change of the AOL people from the "big" list to a special list JUST because AOL hasn't enough brains to provide a state of the art email reader to its users took almost a week alone), the research finding jokes, the production of the babe and hunk pictures, the processing of the payments from the deluxe/babe members and the sponsors, the keeping of books-- in short -- the running of a successful business. Or, as they call it in most parts of the world: Work.*

Splazz with ptd

My friend I have been recieving your jokes for quite some time now and I must say this one thing. THEY SUCK I CAN'T BELIEVE YOU WOULD SEND SUCH SHIT THREWTHE EMAIL. IT IS A WASTE OF GOOD BANDWIDTH. AND AS FOR YOU AREJACKASS OF THE HIGHEST ORDER AND I JUST HAVE ONE LAST THING TOSAY.....................................
keep up the good work I love

Eb with hotmail

Dear Joke Man,

I received the 'joke a day' issue(January 27, 1999), and i was just wondering if this is true...

"WARNING! PLEASE READ IMMEDIATELY! THIS IS SERIOUS!

If you get an envelope from a company called the Internal Revenue Service," DO NOT OPEN IT! This group operates a scam around this time every year . . .

God, shouldn't there be an intelligence test to buy a computer?

Icanfix with AOL

Damn, Chief, don't you ever let up on us AOLiens???

Just as soon as the majority of y'all start showing some sense I'll let up on y'all. :)

But I gotta tell you, I'm beginning to see a new subset of people who REALLY have no business near a keyboard: WebTV. Good Lord, makes the average AOLien look like someone intelligent enough to have jokeaday.com as their email domain.

"Two prostitutes were walking the boulevard . . ."

Two prostitutes were walking the boulevard talking about "business" when a police car went screaming by them with its sirens going and lights flashing. After it had passed, one hooker turned to the other and asked "Hey, you ever been picked up by the fuzz?" "No," the other replied, "but I've been swung around by my tits once or twice."

A Chinese man had three daughters. He asked his eldest daughter what kind of man she would like to marry.

"I would like to marry a man with three dragons on his chest," said the eldest daughter.

He then asked his second daughter whom she would like to marry.

"I would like to marry a man with two dragons on his chest," said the second daughter.

He finally asked his youngest daughter whom she would like to marry.

"I would like to marry a man with one draggin' on the ground," said the youngest daughter.

Boss, to four of his employees: "I'm really sorry, but I'm going to have to let one of you go."

Black Employee: "I'm a protected minority."

Female Employee: "And I'm a woman."

Oldest Employee: "Fire me, buster, and I'll hit you with an age discrimination suit so fast it'll make your head spin."

To which they all turn to look at the helpless young, white, male employee, who thinks a moment, then responds: "I think I might be gay. . ."

A belligerent drunk walks into a bar and hollers: "I can lick any man in the place!"

The nearest customer looks him up and down, then says: "Crude, but direct. Tell me, is this your first time in a gay bar?"

Amanpreet reports for his final exam. The exam consists of nothing but true or false type questions.

He takes his seat, gets the test, stares at the questions for five minutes, and then in a fit of inspiration takes his wallet out, removes a coin, and starts tossing the coin. For "Heads" he marks "True" and for "Tails" he marks "False."

Within half an hour, Amanpreet is all done whereas the rest of the class is sweating it out. During the last few minutes, he is seen desperately throwing the coin, swearing and sweating.

The moderator, a little alarmed, walks over to him and asks him if he's OK.

Amanpreet spits out, "Yeah, I'm OK. I finished my exam in half an hour -- but I'm not going to have time to check all of these answers!!!"

A secretary, a paralegal and a partner in a city law firm are walking through a park on their way to lunch when they find an antique oil lamp. They rub it and a genie comes out in a puff of smoke. The genie says, "I usually only grant three wishes, so I'll give each of you just one."

"Me first! Me first!" says the secretary. "I want to be in the Bahamas, driving a speedboat, without a care in the world."

Poof! She's gone.

"Me next! Me next!" says the paralegal. "I want to be in Hawaii, relaxing on the beach with my personal masseuse, an endless supply of piña coladas and the love of my life."

Poof! He's gone.

"You're next," the genie says to the partner. The partner says, "I want those two back in the office after lunch."

Two drunks were well into their cups at their favorite watering hole, when one spotted movement along the top of the bar.

"Whazz that?" he asked. "A bug?"

"Izz a Ladybug." his friend replied.

"Damn," the first man marveled, "you have good eyesight!"

At the card shop: A woman was spending a long time looking at the cards, finally shaking her head, "No."

A clerk came over and asked, "May I help you?"

"I don't know," said the woman. "Do you have any 'Sorry I laughed at your dick' cards?"

Memo No. 1:
Effective immediately, the company is adopting Fridays as Casual Day so that employees may express their diversity.

Memo No. 2:

Spandex and leather micro-miniskirts are not appropriate attire for Casual Day. Neither are string ties, rodeo belt buckles or moccasins.

Memo No. 3:
Casual Day refers to dress only, not attitude. When planning Friday's wardrobe, remember image is a key to our success.

Memo No. 4:
A seminar on how to dress for Casual Day will be held at 4 p.m. Friday in the cafeteria. Fashion show to follow. Attendance is mandatory.

Memo No. 5:
As an outgrowth of Friday's seminar, the Committee on Committees has appointed a 14-member Casual Day Task Force to prepare guidelines for proper dress.

Memo No. 6:
The Casual Day Task Force has completed a 30-page manual. A copy of "Relaxing Dress without Relaxing Company Standards" has been mailed to each employee. Please review the chapter "You Are What You Wear" and consult the "home casual" versus "business casual" checklist before leaving for work each Friday. If you have doubts about the appropriateness of an item of clothing, contact your CDTF representative before 7 a.m. on Friday.

Memo No. 7:
Because of lack of participation, Casual Day has been discontinued, effective immediately.

Two gas company servicemen, a senior training supervisor and a young trainee, were out checking meters in a suburban neighborhood. They parked their truck at the end of the alley and worked their way to the other end.

At the last house a woman looking out her kitchen window watched the two men as they checked her gas meter.

Finishing the meter check, the senior supervisor challenged his younger coworker to a foot race down the alley back to the truck to prove that an older guy could outrun a younger one.

As they came running up to the truck, they realized the lady from that last house was huffing and puffing right behind them.

They stopped and asked her what was wrong.

Gasping for breath, she replied, "When I saw two gas men running as hard as you two were, I figured I'd better run too!"

A big-city lawyer was representing the railroad in a lawsuit filed by an old rancher. The rancher's prize bull was missing from the section through which the railroad passed. The rancher only wanted to be paid the fair value of the bull.

The case was scheduled to be tried before the justice of the peace in the back room of the general store. The city-slicker attorney for the railroad immediately cornered the rancher and tried to get him to settle out of court.

He did his best selling job, and finally the rancher agreed to take half of what he was asking.

After the rancher had signed the release and took the check, the young lawyer couldn't resist gloating a little over his success, telling the rancher, "You are really a country hick, old man, but I put one over on you in there. I couldn't have won the case. The engineer was asleep and the fireman was in the caboose when the train went through your ranch that morning. I didn't have one witness to put on the stand. I bluffed you!"

The old rancher replied, "Well, I'll tell you young feller, I was a little worried about winning that case myself, because that durned bull came home this morning."

A mother was preparing pancakes for her sons, Kevin, 5, and Ryan, 3. The boys began to argue over who would get the first pancake.

Their mother saw the opportunity for a moral lesson. "If Jesus were sitting here, He would say, 'Let my brother have the first pancake. I can wait.'"

Kevin turned to his younger brother and said, "Ryan, you be Jesus!"

A tall woman met a midget at a party. The midget was barely three feet tall, but they were attracted to each other.

After a few drinks they went back to the tall woman's apartment.

"I can't imagine what it will be like making love to a midget," said the woman, "especially with the size difference and all."

"Just take off your clothes, lie back on the bed, spread your legs apart and close your eyes," said the midget.

The woman did as she was told and soon she felt the biggest thing she'd ever experienced inside her.

Within a few minutes the woman had climaxed eight times.

"If you think that was good," said the midget with a smirk, "Just wait till I get BOTH legs in there!"

A top Pentagon official was finished with an unusually tiring day, grateful to finally be on his way home. Suddenly he found himself in the middle of a traffic jam. Everything was at a dead stop. He noticed a policeman walking up to the driver's window of each car in front of him, so he rolled his window down, waiting for his turn to get the explanation.

"What's going on up there?" demanded the Pentagon executive to the policeman. "Why are we at a total standstill?"

"Well, sir," replied the policeman, "President Clinton stopped his motorcade in the middle of the road ahead. It seems that he's reached a state of total depression. He's worried about the impeachment trial, he's humiliated over his sexual activities making international headlines, and to top it all off, he's convinced that he'll *never* be able to pay his lawyers what he owes them. He's so down over all of this that he's sitting in front of his vehicle, threatening to douse himself with gasoline and set himself on fire. So, I'm going car to car to take up a collection for him."

"How thoughtful," replied the Pentagon exec. "How much do you have so far?"

"Thirty gallons," responded the policeman, "but a few people are still siphoning."

Bill, Hillary, Al and Tipper are all feeling a little saucy in the family room at the White House. Each couple begins talking about going up to their bedrooms when Al has a great idea and suggests that they exchange partners.

Everyone loves the idea, so they swap partners and head to their bedrooms.

A little while later, Bill hears Hillary screaming in ecstasy.

Bill says, "Wow, I've never been able to make Hillary scream like that!"

To which Al replies, "Yeah, Tipper must be hot tonight!"

Man, am I ever glad I live in the United States of America. Otherwise, my impertinence would have allowed me to meet the business end of a government issued AK-47 on more than one occasion.

A deaf mute walks into a pharmacy to buy condoms. He has difficulty communicating with the pharmacist, and cannot see any condoms on the shelf.

Frustrated, the deaf-mute finally unzips his pants, places his dick on the counter, and puts down a five-dollar bill next to it.

The pharmacist unzips his pants, does the same as the deaf-mute, and then picks up both bills and stuffs them in his pocket. Exasperated, the deaf mute begins to curse the pharmacist wildly in sign language.

"Look," the pharmacist says, "if you can't afford to lose, you shouldn't bet."

A young woman buys a mirror at an antique shop, and hangs it on her bathroom door. One evening, while getting undressed, she playfully says "Mirror, mirror, on my door, make my bust-line forty four." Instantly, there is a brilliant flash of light, and her breasts grow to enormous proportions.

Excitedly, she runs to tell her husband what happened, and in minutes they both return. This time the husband crosses his fingers and says "Mirror, mirror on the door, make my penis touch the floor!" Again, there's a bright flash -- and both his legs fall off.

Two men are in the pub, talking about the lazy shiftless youth of today. They get on to the subject of their sons, and end up arguing over who has the laziest bum for offspring. Neither can believe that anyone could possibly have spawned a bigger layabout than himself, so they place bets and agree to visit each other at home to see just how sluggish each other's lad is.

They go into the first guy's house and there is no sign of the son. "Ah, that's 'cause he's in bed. It's only 10 p.m., and he never gets up before midnight, if he ever gets up at all. I've never even caught him getting up for a leak."

And sure enough the son is in bed, wide awake, remote for the TV in hand. His room stinks.

"Hi, Dad."

"Hi, Son, can you get up outa bed now?"

"No, I'm quite happy here, Dad."

"I'll give you $1000 a week allowance if you do."

"Nah, no thanks. I can't be bothered. I'll just stay here if it's OK."

The first father, is, needless to say, pleased with the display of slothfulness his son has supplied the other guy with. Surely no one can beat that.

"That's nothing," says man #2. "Wait 'til you meet my son."

So they go to his house and the son is lying on the floor by the fireside watching TV. The first guy isn't impressed. "He's bloody hyperactive compared to my son; he's even dressed!"

Then they go closer, and notice that the lad is crying, evidently in some pain. His father is unconcerned, but the first guy says, "What's wrong, lad?"

He wails back, "I'm burning."

A Russian is strolling down the street in Moscow and kicks a bottle lying in the street. Suddenly out of the bottle comes a Genie. The Russian is stunned and the Genie says, "Hello Master, I will grant you one wish, anything you want."

The Russian begins thinking, "Well, I really like drinking vodka."

Finally the Russian says, "I wish to drink vodka whenever I want, so make me piss vodka."

The Genie grants him his wish. When the Russian gets home he gets a glass out of the cupboard and pisses in it. He looks at the glass and it's clear. Looks like vodka. Then he smells the liquid. Smells like vodka. So he takes a taste and it is the best vodka he has ever tasted.

The Russian yells to his wife, "Natasha, Natasha, come quickly!"

She comes running down the hall and the Russian takes another glass out of the cupboard and pisses into it. He tells her to drink, it is vodka. Natasha is reluctant but goes ahead and takes a sip. It is the best vodka she has ever tasted. The two drink and party all night.

The next night the Russian comes home from work and tells his wife to get two glasses out of the cupboard. He proceeds to piss in the two glasses. The result is the same, the vodka is excellent and the couple drinks until the sun comes up.

Finally Friday night comes and the Russian comes home and tells his wife, "Natasha, grab one glass from the cupboard and we will drink vodka."

His wife gets the glass from the cupboard and sets it on the table. The Russian begins to piss in the glass and when he fills it his wife asks him, "But Boris, why do we need only one glass?"

Boris raises the glass and says, "Because tonight, my love, you drink from the bottle."

A man rushes into his house and yells to his wife, "Martha, pack up your things. I just won the California lottery!"

Martha replies, "Shall I pack for warm weather or cold?"

The man responds, "I don't care. Just so long as you're out of the house by noon!"

A man goes skydiving for the first time. After listening to the instructor for what seems like days, he is ready to go.

Excited, he jumps out of the airplane. After a bit, he pulls the ripcord. Nothing happens.

He tries again. Still nothing.

He starts to panic, but remembers his back-up chute. He pulls that cord. Nothing happens. He frantically begins pulling both cords, but to no avail.

Suddenly, he looks down and he can't believe his eyes. Another man is in the air with him, but this guy is going *up*!

Just as the other guy passes by, the skydiver -- by this time scared out of his wits -- yells, "Hey, do you know anything about skydiving?"

The other guy yells back, "No! Do you know anything about gas stoves?"

Bob, an experienced sky diver, was getting ready for a jump one day when he spotted another man outfitted to dive wearing dark glasses, carrying a white cane and holding a seeing-eye dog by a leash. Shocked that the blind man was also going to jump, Bob struck up a conversation, expressing his admiration for the man's courage. Then, curious, he asked, "How do you know when the ground is getting close?"

"Easy," replied the blind man. "The leash goes slack."

A husband and his wife advertised for a live-in maid to cook and do the housework. They hired a lovely lass for the job.

She worked out fine, was a good cook, was polite, and kept the house neat. One day, after about six months, she came in and said she would have to quit.

"But why?" asked the disappointed wife.

She hemmed and hawed and said she didn't want to say, but the wife was persistent, so finally she said, "Well, on my day off a couple of months ago I met this good-looking fellow from over in the next county, and well, I'm pregnant."

The wife said, "Look, we don't want to lose you. My husband and I don't have any children, and we'll adopt your baby if you will stay."

She talked to her husband; he agreed, and the maid said she would stay. The baby came, they adopted it, and all went well.

After several months though, the maid came in again and said that she would have to quit. The wife questioned her, found out that she was pregnant again, talked to her husband, and offered to adopt the baby if she would stay. She agreed, had the baby, they adopted it, and life went on as usual.

In a few months, however, she again said she would have to leave. Same thing. She was pregnant. They made the same offer, she agreed, and they adopted the third baby. She worked for a week or two, but then said, "I am definitely leaving this time."

"Don't tell me you're pregnant again?" asked the lady of the house.

"No," she said, "there are just too many kids here to pick up after."

"Take me off your mailing list or I'll shoot myself."

wilderrv with ozarks.net
Your stories are fucking stupid, and your jokes are lame. Take me off your mailing list or I'll shoot myself.

Well, since I won't be taking you off the list, where should we send flowers for the funeral?

Mike with Juno
This is Mike. You probabaly don't reconize me, I only wrote back once before. I'm justhere to say that most of what you send could be better, some of your jokes just plain bite. But a lot are just ruind by your presentation. I'm note sure if it was you, but one of these lists really botched 51 days. I've heard that joke over 59 times and that was the worst version yet. (I am considerd a sort of joke critic) Now you also screwed up many other jokes but I'll emficise on this one.

Three blonds walk into a bar chanting 51 DAYS 51 DAYS. Then 7 more blonds come inchanting 51 DAYS 51 DAYS. After about an hour of steady increase in blonds Hefinnaly pulls one of the festive girls from the crowd of drunk partying babes revolvingaroun a beutifly framed puzzle of Kermit the frog and asks her what is going on. SheLaughs back, "Well, like we were tired of people think'n us blonds are dumb and all that,so we got 150 of us togeather to prove them wrong so we got a puzzle that said 2 to 4years, and we all worked night and day and it only took us 51 DAYS!!!!!!!"

Hi Mike:

*Why the hell are you writing **me** on this? I never told that joke.*

You say that my presentation sucks. I've got to tell you, I've read this joke a thousand times and yours is, by far, the worst rendition of it I've ever seen.

Until you learn how to properly format paragraphs, how to spell, and the proper use of English, I'd strongly suggest you retire your "joke critic" title.

Ray
Joke A Day

Mimi with New Media
You appear to be a conceited, egotistical, sarcastic, condescending, AOL-hating, self-serving prick. I love that in a man ! I am really turned on right now.

Rachael with Yahoo
Dearest Ray,

Could the gods have created a more perfect male specimen of a human being? You're handsome and intelligent and, above all, funny! Just reading what you have to say every day on your website makes me want you even more. I don't care that you're old and I'm only 15... please be my Valentine!

(Incidentally, I'm really 19 and have a boyfriend, but I'm trying damn hard to make your "Letters to JAD" section. How am I doing? ,))

-Rachael

Gee, Rach, I'm not sure you're sucking up enough. The odds of your letter ever reaching the letters page are pretty remote . . .

Ray
Joke A Day

P.S. I'm old???

Heckler with AOL

no offense , but your jokes are kinda lame, id like to get some more dirty jokes, like yesterdays

No offense, but people from AOL are pretty lame. I'd like to get less mail -- like yesterday.

listen, i didnt want to start being email buddies, i just wanted off the mailing list

Listen, I didn't want to be a babysitting service to AOL idiots. I just wanted to run a little business that catered to people who knew how to read. You're NOT in that subset of humanity, obviously. (Are these words too big for you? Too many syllables?)

if you have a joke mail for just dirty jokes, count me in , buy everything else i dont like

*I **do** have a listing for just AOL people just like you.*

Send an email to:
iamacluelessmoronandcantfollowdirectionsworthshit@jokeaday.com

listen bitch, dont fuck with me , take me off your stupid list, and i dont give a shit aboutyour little buisiness that you run from your packard bell. please leave me alone and stop cluttering my mailbox with stupid stolen jokes that you got from other sites!!! Thank you

P.S - is that too hard to understand jackass

a little later he sent this

I'm sorry, please unsubscribe me.

"Marine biology researchers have developed a new method to fend off shark attacks . . ."

"Marine biology researchers have developed a new method to fend off shark attacks. If you are diving and are approached by a shark, they recommend that you swim towards it aggressively and punch it in the nose as hard as possible."

"If this doesn't work, beat the shark with your stump."

What goes "clip-clop clip-clop clip-clop clip-clop clip-clop bang bang bang bang bang bang bang clip-clop clip-clop clip-clop clip-clop clip-clop"?

An Amish drive-by shooting.

"I haven't sold one tractor all month," a tractor salesman tells his friend.

"That's nothing compared to my problem," his buddy replies. "I was milking my cow when its tail whips around and hits me in the forehead, so I grabbed some string and tied its tail up to the rafters. Then I go back to milk it and it kicks me in the head with its right hind leg, so I grab some rope and tie its one leg up to the rafters. I go back to try and milk it again when it kicks me in the head with its left hind leg, so I tie its other leg up to the rafters. "

"Then my wife comes walking in and I'll tell ya, if you can convince her that I was trying to milk that cow, I'll buy a tractor off ya."
When my aunt backed the family van into the garage, she accidentally knocked off a side mirror. "Someone hit the van while I was shopping

at the mall," she told my uncle upon his return from the office. "The culprit didn't even leave a note. Can you imagine the nerve?"

"The guy had more nerve than you think," my uncle replied. "He even followed you and put the broken glass in our garage."

A man goes into a drug store and asks the cashier for some rubbers. The cashier asks, "What size?"

The man replies, "Size? I didn't know they came in sizes."

"Yes, they do," she says, "What size do you want?"

"Well, gee, I don't know," the man answers.

The lady is used to this, so she tells him to go to the back yard and measure his dick by sticking it into each of the three holes in the fence. While the man is back there, the lady sneaks around to the other side of the fence and spreads her legs behind each hole as the man tests it. When they return, the cashier asks, "What will it be? Small, medium, or large?"

The man replies, "To hell with the rubbers! Give me a hundred feet of that fence back there!"

A man is having problems with his dick, which certainly has seen better times. He consults a doctor, who, after a couple of tests, says, "Sorry, but you've overdone it the last 20 years, your dick is burned out; you won't be able to make love more than 30 times!"

The man walks home (deeply depressed, of course); his wife is already expecting him at the front door and asks him what the doctor said concerning his problem. He tells her what the doc told him.

She says: "Oh my God, only 30 more times! We shouldn't waste that; we should make a list!" He replies, "Yes, I already made a list on the way home. Sorry, your name isn't on it!"

One day a nun was fishing and caught a huge, strange-looking fish.

A man was walking by and said, "WOW!! What a nice Gauddam Fish!" The sister said, "Sir, you shouldn't use God's name in vain." The man said, "But that's the SPECIES of the fish -- a Gauddam Fish."

The sister said, "Oh, OK." She took the fish back home and said, "Mother Superior, look at the Gauddam Fish I caught."

Shocked, the Mother Superior said, "Sister, you know better than that." The nun said, "That's the species of it -- a Gauddam Fish."

So the Mother Superior said, "Well, give me the Gauddam Fish and I'll clean it."

While she was cleaning the fish, Monsignor walked in and Mother Superior said, "Monsignor, look at the Gauddam Fish that the sister caught." Nearly fainting, Monsignor said, "Mother Superior, you shouldn't talk like that!" Mother Superior said, "But that's the species of it -- a Gauddam Fish." Monsignor said, "Well, give me the Gauddam Fish and I'll cook it."

That evening at supper there was a new priest at the table, and he said, "Wow, what a nice fish." In reply, the sister said, "Thank you, I caught the Gauddam Fish." And Mother Superior said, "I cleaned the Gauddam Fish." And Monsignor said, "I cooked the Gauddam Fish."

The priest looked around in disbelief, quite shocked, and said, "I LIKE THIS FUCKING PLACE ALREADY!"

The teacher had given the class an assignment. He stressed the importance of this particular assignment, and that no excuses would be accepted except illness (with a medical certificate) or a death in the immediate family (with a note from that member). A smart-ass student piped up:

"What about extreme sexual exhaustion, sir?"

The class broke up laughing, and when they settled down the teacher responded with: "Well, I guess you'll have to learn to write with your other hand."

A cowboy is riding across the plains of the Old West, when Indians capture him. The tribe puts him on trial for crimes against the Indian Nation, and he is found guilty.

"You have been sentenced to death," said the Chief, "but, as is our custom, you have three wishes to make as your last requests."

The cowboy thought for a minute and said, "Well, for my first wish, I'll need my horse."

"Give him his horse," said the Chief.

The cowboy whispered something into the horse's ear, and the horse took off like a shot across the prairie. Twenty minutes later, the horse returned with a beautiful blonde woman on its back. The cowboy looked at this, shrugged his shoulders, and helped the young lady off the horse. He then took her into the woods.

"Second wish," said the Chief.

"I'll need my horse again," said the cowboy.

"Give him his horse," said the Chief.

Once again, the cowboy whispered into the horse's ear, and once again the horse rode off over the prairie. Thirty minutes later, the horse returned with a beautiful redhead on its back.

The cowboy looked up and shrugged, helped the young lady off the horse, and went into the woods.

"This is your last wish," said the Chief, "make it a good one."

"I'll need my horse again."

"Give him his horse," said the Chief.

The cowboy grabbed each side of the horse's head and put his face right up to the horse's.

"Look, it's POSSE, OK? POSSE!!!"

This is another favorite of mine to tell in person. I don't know why I felt the need to break in here and tell you this. Actually, I do know the reason, but it has nothing to do with this book.

If you're reading this book and you can manage to get me an introduction to Kristina Abernathy of the Weather Channel, I'd be indebted to you forever. What a babe and a half. Brains. Beauty. And the cutest Southern accent ever.

A baby polar bear goes up to his mother and says, "Mom, am I a polar bear?"

His mother says, "Of course you're a polar bear. I'm a polar bear and your father's a polar bear."

The cub says, "But am I one-hundred percent pure polar bear?"

She says, "Go ask your old man."

The baby polar bear goes up to his father and says, "Pop, am I a polar bear? I mean, one-hundred percent pure polar bear?"

His father says, "Of course you're a polar bear. I'm a polar bear, your mother's a polar bear, both my parents were polar bears, both of your mother's parents were polar bears, all of our grandparents, both sides, were polar bears, yes, you're one-hundred percent pure polar bear. Why do you ask?"

The cub says, "Because I'm fucking freezing."

A woman has twins, and gives them up for adoption. One of them goes to a family in Egypt, and is named "Amal." The other goes to a family in Spain; they name him "Juan."

Years later, Juan sends a picture of himself to his mom. Upon receiving the picture, she tells her husband that she wishes she also had a picture of Amal. Her husband responds, "But they are twins--if you've seen Juan, you've seen Amal."

Two little boys were watching a dog clean himself.

They watched him for quite awhile until finally one of the boys said, "I wish I could do that."

The other little boy said, "He'd bite you."

Did ya hear. . . ?
Buckwheat attended the Million Man March and was motivated to convert to the Muslim faith. His new Muslim name is Kareem-A-Wheat.

OK, we all know that 666 is the Number of the Beast. But did you know:

$665.95 - Retail price of the Beast

$699.25 - Price of the Beast plus 5% sales tax

$769.95 - Price of the Beast with all accessories and replacement soul

$766.25 - Price of the Beast with extended 6 year 66,000 mile warranty

$656.66 – Wal-Mart price of the Beast

00666 - Zip code of the Beast

1-900-666-0666 - Live Beasts! One-on-one pacts! Call Now! $6.66/minute. Over 18 please.

Route 666 - Highway of the Beast

666 F - Oven temperature for roast Beast

666(k) - Retirement plan of the Beast

6.66 % - 5 year CD interest rate at First Beast National Bank, $666 minimum deposit

i66686 - CPU of the Beast

666i - BMW of the Beast

668 - Next-door neighbor of the Beast

Don't forget 66... uhhh -- the Blonde Beast

Two car salesmen were sitting at the bar. One complained to the other, "Boy, business sucks. If I don't sell more cars this month, I'm going to lose my fucking ass." Too late he noticed a beautiful blonde sitting two stools away.

Immediately, he apologized for his bad language. "That's OK," the blonde replied, "If I don't sell more ass this month, I'm going to lose my fucking car."

An Army grunt stands in the rain with a 35 lb. pack on his back, 15 lb. weapon in hand, after marching 12 miles, and says "God, this is SHIT."

An Army Airborne grunt stands in the rain with a 45 lb. pack on his back, weapon in hand, after jumping from an airplane and marching 18 miles, and says with a smile, "God, this is THE shit."

An Army Airborne Ranger lies in the mud, 55 lb. pack on his back, weapon in hand, after jumping from a plane into the swamp and marching 25 miles at night past the enemy, and says with a grin, "God, I LOVE this shit!"

An Army Green Beret, Airborne/Ranger/Pathfinder qualified, kneels up to his nose in the stinking, infested mud of a swamp with a 65 lb. pack on his back and a weapon in both hands after jumping from an airplane into the ocean, swimming 10 miles to the swamp and killing an alligator, then crawling 30 miles through the brush to assault the enemy camp. He says with a passionate snarl, "God, gimmee some MORE of this shit!"

An Air Force cadet sits in an easy chair in his air-conditioned, carpeted room and says, "The cable's out? What kind of shit is that?!?"

The very young couple, having limited funds, returned to her parents' after the wedding for their honeymoon night. The next morning the family gathered for breakfast and lunch without them.

When it came time for the evening meal, the father asked of his wife and their 8-year-old son, "Have any of you seen the newlyweds?"

The mother replied she had not seen her daughter and new son-in-law. The bride's younger brother replied that he had seen his new brother-in-law about 10 p.m. when he stuck his head out the door and asked him if he knew where there was any Vaseline. To which the young lad further added that since he could not find any Vaseline that he had given him his model airplane glue.

This fellow was screwing his best friend's wife when he suddenly stopped and sat on the edge of the bed, holding his head in his hands.

"What the hell has happened to you?" the lady asked.

"I feel like a regular son of a bitch, getting my best friend's pussy," the man moaned.

The lady reached over and patted him on the back. "Well, if that's all it is, you can stop worrying," she said. "You're not getting his pussy. His pussy is five to six inches deeper."

Did you ever hear the Richard Pryor routine where he talked about how "cool" women get when you argue with them?

"I'll just go find me some 'new' pussy!"
"If you had another inch on your dick you could find some new pussy here!"

How is a penis like fishing?
The small ones you throw back.
The medium ones you eat.
And the large ones you mount!

"Sir, if you were my husband, I would poison your drink."   --Lady Astor to Winston Churchill

"Madam, if you were my wife, I would drink it." --His reply

I read a book called "Wipeouts" once. It was all about the art of insulting people. Winston Churchill was a master. For instance, George Bernard Shaw sent him two tickets to Shaw's new play. Inside the ticket envelope Shaw had written, "I've enclosed two tickets. Bring a friend, if you have one." Churchill wrote back, "Can't make it first night. Will be there second night -- if you have one."

"I can never fool my wife," the first man complained. "I turn off the car's engine and coast into the garage, take off my shoes, sneak upstairs, and undress in the bathroom. But she always wakes up and yells at me for being out so late and leaving her alone."

"You got the wrong technique, my friend," his buddy replied. "I roar into the garage, slam the door, stomp up the steps, rub my hand on her ass and say, 'How about a little?' She always pretends to be asleep."

A priest was hearing confession one evening when an elderly gentleman entered the confessional.

"Forgive me Father for I have sinned. I'm 80 years old and have been faithful to my wife for all 60 years of our marriage. That all ended last night when I spent the evening with 2 attractive twins who had just moved into our building."

"Our God is a merciful God. Tell me, when was your last confession?"

"Never. I'm Jewish."

"Then why are you telling me your confession?"

"Are you kidding? At my age, I'm telling EVERYONE!!"

An Australian was walking down a country road in New Zealand, when he happened to glance over the fence and see a farmer goin' at it with a sheep. The Aussie is quite taken aback by this, so he climbs the fence and walks over to the farmer. He taps him on the shoulder and says, "You know mate, back home, we shear those!"

The New Zealander looks frantically around and says, "I'm not bloody SHEARING this with no one!"

(helps to imagine a New Zealand accent . . .)

Lying in the hospital bed, the dying man began to flail about and make motions as if he would like to speak. The priest, keeping watch at the side of his bed leaned over quietly and asked, "Do you have something you would like to say?"

The man nodded to the affirmative, and the priest handed him a pad and pen. "I know you can't speak, but use this to write a note and I will give it to your wife. She's waiting just outside."

Gathering his last bit of strength, the man took them and scrawled his message upon the pad, which he stuffed into the priest's hands. Then, moments later, the man died.

After administering the last rites, the priest left to break the sad news to the wife. After consoling her a bit, the priest handed her the note. "Here were his last words. Just before passing on, he wrote this message to you."

The wife tearfully opened the note, which read:

"GET OFF MY *!#%*!!**$%^! OXYGEN HOSE!!"

There is this American tourist on a trip around Ireland.

When the tour arrives at Belfast he decides to go for a stroll with the aim of taking in this new culture. After he's been walking for a while someone rushes up behind him and sticks a gun in his back.

The gunman says to the tourist, "Are you Catholic or Protestant?"

The American thinks to himself, "If I say I'm Catholic, this guy is sure to be Protestant. If I say I'm Protestant, he's sure to be Catholic. Either way I'm dead."

Then he has a brainstorm. He says to the gunman, "Actually, I'm Jewish."

The gunman behind him cocks the trigger and replies, "Gee, I must be the luckiest Arab in Ireland."

*Oh, man, did I ever hear about **that** joke. Curiously enough, the biggest group of people that complained were the Southern Baptists. (I'm kidding . . .)*

"And as for you, you good for nothing computer geek, your jokes suck!"

Snookumska at AOL
Listen asshole, it's people like you that make this world so much more pleasant to live in. #1. I didn't put myself on your list, and #2. Now that I know how to take my name of this list I have. And as for my intelligence for all you know I may have a PHD. And as for you, you good for nothing computer geek, your jokes suck!

*You're right, it's people like me who make this world a **better** place to live in.*

#1. The ONLY way you could have been placed on this list WITHOUT your permission is if you gave control of your email to someone else. Your being on AOL means you have ZERO brains. Giving control of your email address, for you, is a distinct possibility. Only idiots allow other people to use their email accounts. You've done nothing but display you're an idiot.

*#2. "Ph.D." is the **proper** way to put it. If you had one, you'd know that. About the only thing you have a degree in is stupidity.*

*You're only upset that I made you actually DO something (i.e., read and follow the unsubscribe instructions) instead of allowing you to make **me** do the work. This is why you're acting like a 5-year-old with the name-calling.*

I'm glad you figured out the unsub instructions. Folks like you I don't need on the list.

abdikarim with psu.edu
someone send me a card and I can't find the card on your web. I thing you guys can do little better than this, you give me a number and web

address to locard my greeting card, however the only thing on that web side is some joke. please stop making people.............

Stop making people? Hell, don't you know the best part about kids is making 'em?

In the meantime, you and Amanpreet hook up until you've sufficiently learned enough of the English language to be able to read and follow directions.

You just lost ONE! Next time I will use OTHER free greeting card services! However, I feel bad for your sponsor because your not helping them by responding your customers e-mail this way.. By the way, I speak three other languages GERMAN, ARABIC and ENGLISH. And I am here to STAY just like your grandfather did.

My grandfather was already here, thank you, but I don't know what that has to do with learning English. (He could read and write and follow directions, though.)

Trust me when I tell you that I won't miss you.

Ms. Ferrari with netscape *(in response to my letter saying we don't offer a "Hunk A Day" Subscription)*
thats not fair!!!!!!!

WE WANT HUNKS DAMMIT!!!!!!!!!!!! WOMAN RIGHTS!!!!!!!!

You have no rights here.

This is Joke A Day Land and I am the Ruler Over All.

But crossing my palm with some silver, say to the tune of $500 a month, will buy your way into the Kingdom of the Hunks, m'lady.

Ray
Joke A Day

Idiot chick with AOL
i think you're funny:)

*Sigh -- someone from AOL **finally** shows some intelligence and her nick is
"idiotchick"...*

Dee with Juno
Ray
... A question for you... How come your "blonde" awards are names the Judi &Jan awards... Instead of Barbra & Bill or something... I was extremely curious about that.
Love, Dee

*Dee, you **really** should get an Internet connection so you can go to the web page and find the answers to this stuff, ma'am.*

I have no desire to get an "internet cannection." I think those things are a conspiracy by the government in an attempt to ruin the morals of our society.
Love,Dee

Sandy with netcenter
Dear Ray,

I admire the way you can flame people. I thought I encountered the stupidest people ever, (working in a supermarket) but after reading some of the letters you get, I stand corrected. I take my hat off to you. I wish sometimes I could tell people off the way you do, but I can't -- customer service and all that. It is so tiring to have to put up with idiots. Keep up the good fight.

All hail Ray the God of Jokes and Flames.

You know, Rhonda, I think my most valuable service is stomping on idiots so folks like you who are bound by "customer service" can live vicariously through the letters page. I can't tell you how many letters I get just like that -- "Man, I had this bonehead on the phone today and I just WISH I could say to him the stuff you get to say . . ."   :)

Believe me, I've spent my whole professional career in customer service roles, and I've got permanent teeth marks in my tongue from biting it for so many years.

Take care and thanks for writing.

Ray
Joke A Day

"This married man goes to confessional . . ."

This married man goes to confessional and he tells the priest, "I had an affair with a woman . . . almost." The priest asks, "What do you mean, almost?"

The man says "Well, we got undressed and rubbed together but then I stopped." The priest replies, "Rubbing together is the same as putting it in. You're not to go near that woman again; now say five Hail Marys and put $50 in the poor box."

The man leaves confessional, goes over and says his prayers, then walks over to the poor box. He pauses for a moment and then starts to leave. The priest, who was watching him, quickly runs over to him and says "I saw that! You didn't put any money in the poor box!"

The man replied, "Well, Father, I rubbed up against it, and you said it was the same as putting it in!"

A certain young man finally won a date with the blonde female of somewhat questionable morals who lived in his apartment complex. To prepare for his big date, the young man went up on to the roof of his apartment building in order to tan himself.

Not wanting any tan lines to show, he sunbathed in the nude.

Unfortunately, the young man fell asleep while on the roof, and managed to get a sunburn on his "tool of the trade." But he was determined not to miss his date, so he put some lotion on his manhood and wrapped it in gauze.

The blonde showed up for the date at his apartment, and the young man treated her to a home-cooked dinner, after which they went into the living room to watch a movie. During the movie, however, the young man's sunburn started acting up again. He asked to be excused, went into the kitchen, and poured a tall, cool glass of milk.

He then placed his sunburned member in the milk and experienced immediate relief of his pain. The blonde, however, wondering what he was doing, wandered into the kitchen to see him with his Johnson immersed in a glass of milk.

Upon seeing this, the blonde exclaimed, "So that's how you guys load those things!"

"I'd like my money back, please."

"Excuse me?"

"I'd like my money back, please. Your advertisement said 'Money refunded if not satisfactory.'"

"Oh, I'm afraid that is not possible. You see, your money was quite satisfactory, thank you."

This is what I tell people who place ads with me.

This 85-year-old couple, having been married almost 60 years, had died in a car crash. They had been in good health the last ten years, mainly due to her interest in health food, and exercise.

When they reached the pearly gates, St. Peter took them to their mansion, which was decked out with a beautiful kitchen, master bath suite and Jacuzzi.

As they "oohed" and "aahed," the old man asked Peter how much all this was going to cost.

"It's free," Peter replied. "This is Heaven."

Next they went out back to survey the championship golf course that the home backed up to. They would have golfing privileges every day and each week the course changed to a new one representing the great golf courses on earth.

The old man asked, "What are the green fees?"

Peter's reply, "This is Heaven; you play for free."

Next they went to the clubhouse and saw the lavish buffet lunch with the cuisines of the world laid out.

"How much to eat?" asked the old man.

"Don't you understand yet? This is Heaven; it is free!" Peter replied with some exasperation.

"Well, where are the low fat and low cholesterol tables?" the old man asked timidly.

Peter lectured, "That's the best part. You can eat as much as you like of whatever you like and you never get fat and you never get sick. This is Heaven."

With that the old man went into a fit of anger, throwing down his hat and stomping on it, and shrieking wildly.

Peter and his wife both tried to calm him down, asking him what was wrong. The old man looked at his wife and said, "This is all your fault. If it weren't for your blasted bran muffins, I could have been here ten years ago!"

While cruising at 40,000 feet, the airplane shuddered and Mr. Benson looked out the window.

"Good Lord!" he screamed. "One of the engines just blew up!"

Other passengers left their seats and came running over; suddenly the aircraft was rocked by a second blast as yet another engine exploded on the other side.

The passengers were in a panic now, and even the stewardesses couldn't maintain order.   Just then, standing tall and smiling confidently, the pilot strode from the cockpit and assured everyone that there was nothing to worry about. His words and demeanor seemed to make most of the passengers feel better, and they sat down as the pilot calmly walked to the door of the aircraft. There, he grabbed several packages from under the seats and began handing them to the flight attendants.

All the crewmembers attached the packages to their backs.

"Say," spoke up an alert passenger, "aren't those parachutes?"

The pilot said they were.

The passenger went on, "But I thought you said there was nothing to worry about?"

"There isn't," replied the pilot as a third engine exploded. "We're going to get help."

Preacher: "How come I never see you in church anymore, Morris?"

Morris: "There are too many hypocrites there, Reverend."

Preacher: "Don't worry, Morris; there's always room for one more."

One day, Grandma sent her grandson Johnny down to the water hole to get some water for cooking dinner. As he was dipping the bucket in, he saw two big eyes looking back at him. He dropped the bucket and hightailed it for Grandma's kitchen.

"Well now, where's my bucket and where's my water?" Grandma asked him.

"I can't get any water from that water hole, Grandma," exclaimed Johnny. "There's a BIG ol' alligator down there!"

"Now don't you mind that ol' alligator, Johnny. He's been there for a few years now, and he's never hurt no one. Why, he's probably as scared of you as you are of him!"

"Well, Grandma," replied Johnny, "if he's as scared of me as I am of him, then that water ain't fit to drink!"

A meat counter clerk, who had had a particularly good day, proudly flipped his last chicken on a scale and weighed it. "That will be $6.35," he told the customer.

"That really is a little too small," said the woman. "Don't you have anything larger?"

Hesitating, but thinking fast, the clerk returned the chicken to the refrigerator, paused a moment, then took it out again.

"This one," he said faintly, " will be $6.65."

The woman paused for a moment, then made her decision. "I know what," she said, "I'll take both of them!"

Two men are having a beer, and the conversation turns to women and sex, as it often does.

"Do you know why women fake orgasm?" the younger one asks.

"Yes," says the other man. "They still don't realize that we don't care."

Leroy and Jasper have been promoted from privates to sergeants. Not long after, they're out for a walk and Leroy says, "Hey, Jasper, there's the Officers' Club. Let's you and me stop in."

"But we's privates," protests Jasper.

"We's sergeants now," says Leroy, pulling him inside. "Now, Jasper, I'se gonna sit down and have me a drink." "But we's privates," says Jasper.

"You blind?" asks Leroy, pointing at his stripes. "We's sergeants now."

So they have their drink, and pretty soon a hooker comes up to Leroy. "You're cute," she says, "and I'd like to screw you, but I've got a bad case of gonorrhea."

Leroy pulls his friend to the side and whispers, "Jasper, go look in the dictionary and see what 'gonorrhea' means. If it's OK, give me the okay sign." So Jasper goes to look it up, comes back, and gives Leroy the big OK sign. Three weeks later Leroy is laid up in the infirmary with a terrible case of gonorrhea.

"Jasper," he says, "what fo' you give me the OK?" "Well, Leroy, in the dictionary, it say gonorrhea affects only the privates." He points to his stripes. "But we's sergeants now."

Brenda, pregnant with her first child, was paying a visit to her obstetrician's office. When the exam was over, she shyly began, "My husband wants me to ask you . . ."

"I know, I know." the doctor said, placing a reassuring hand on her shoulder, "I get asked that all the time. Sex is fine until late in the pregnancy."

"No, that's not it at all." Brenda confessed. "He wants to know if I can still mow the lawn."

A worried father confronted his daughter one night. "I don't like that new boyfriend, he's rough and common and bloody stupid with it."

"Oh no, Daddy," the daughter replied, "Fred's ever so clever. We've only been going out nine weeks and he's cured me of that illness I used to get once a month."

God gave me two daughters. He did it to remind me that He was in charge. He did it because I've been such a hound all of my life. (Note my previous comments about Kristina Abernathy.)

*But God knows that **I** know what goes on in little boys' minds. And He knows I don't want them thinking that about my little girls. Aaaargh.*

This fellow who had spent his whole life in the desert comes to visit a friend. He'd never seen a train or the tracks they run on.

While standing in the middle of the RR tracks one day, he hears this whistle -- Whooee da Whoee! -- but doesn't know what it is.

Predictably, he's hit -- but only a glancing blow -- and is thrown, ass-over-teakettle, to the side of the tracks, with some minor internal injuries, a few broken bones, and some bruises.

After weeks in the hospital recovering, he's at his friend's house attending a party one evening. While in the kitchen, he suddenly hears the teakettle whistling. He grabs a baseball bat from the nearby closet and proceeds to batter and bash the teakettle into an unrecognizable lump of metal. His friend, hearing the ruckus, rushes into the kitchen, sees what's happened and asks the desert man: "Why'd you ruin my good tea kettle?"

The desert man replies, "Man, you gotta kill these things when they're small."

While leading a party of Girl Scouts through the woods in silent Indian fashion, the troop leader suddenly came upon a clearing where a young couple was engaged in "69."

"Back, ladies, back!" cried the leader, "There's a very dangerous beast out there!" But it was too late. Several of her charges had more-or-less seen all.

They asked their leader what was happening.

"Well, if you, uhh, must know, they were practicing a brand-new form of artificial respiration."

"WOW!" exclaimed the oldest of the group. "I know which merit badge I'm gonna try for next."

What did Queen Elizabeth II say to O.J. Simpson?
"That's how it's done."

An airline pilot wrote that on this particular flight he had hammered his ship into the runway really hard. The airline had a policy which required the first officer to stand at the door while the passengers exited, give a smile, and a "Thanks for flying XYZ airline." He said that in light of his bad landing, he had a hard time looking the passengers in the eye, thinking that someone would have a smart comment, but no one seemed annoyed.

Finally everyone had gotten off except for one little old lady walking with a cane. She approached and asked, conspiratorially, "Sonny, mind if I ask you a question?"

"Why, no, Ma'am, what is it?"

"Did we land or were we shot down?"

This guy was applying for a job as a flagman/switch operator on the railroad. The engineer was conducting the interview. "What would you do if the Northern Express was heading north on Track 1 and the Southern Central was heading south on Track 1?"

The guy thought. "Well, I'd call my brother."

The engineer just sat there for a second. *"Why* would you call your brother???"

"He's never seen a train wreck before."

Did you hear about the Veterinarian and the Taxidermist who combined their business? Their slogan:

"Either way you get your pet back."

This construction worker had climbed 20 stories to the job site. Once there he'd asked the foreman if he could go back down to take a leak. Not wanting to lose the time, the foreman balanced one I-beam across another, stood on one end, and told the worker to walk out to the other end to pee.

While the worker was doing his business, the phone rang. The foreman, forgetting what he was doing, stepped off the I-beam and the worker plunged 20 stories to his death.

The next week the safety inspectors came by to conduct a routine investigation into the accident. They talked to the ground crew.

"I think it was sex-related," offered one of the crew.

"Sex-related? How do you figure that?" said the investigator.

"Well, what made me look up was this guy coming down, dick in his hand, screaming, 'where did that cocksucker go???'"

Why do men snore when they lie on their backs? Because their balls fall over their asshole and they vapor lock.

An older man wearing a stovepipe hat, a waistcoat and a phony beard sat down at a bar and ordered a drink. As the bartender set it down, he asked, "Going to a party?"

"Yeah," the man answered, "I'm supposed to come dressed as my love life."

"But you look like Abe Lincoln." protested the barkeep.

"That's right. My last four scores were seven years ago."

Two Polish guys were going to Warsaw on their first train trip. A vendor came down the corridor selling bananas, which they'd never seen before. Each bought one.

The first one eagerly peeled the banana and bit into it just as the train went into a tunnel. When the train emerged from the tunnel, he looked across to his friend and said, "I wouldn't eat that if I were you."

"Why not?"

"I took one bite and went blind for half a minute."

A middle aged woman stood watching a little boy standing on the curb, smoking a cigarette and drinking from a bottle of Scotch. Finally, unable to bear it any longer, she stalked up to the lad and demanded, "Why aren't you in school at this time of day?"

"Hell, lady," said the boy, gulping from the bottle, "I'm only four years old."

A husband and wife noticed that their little boy's penis was a little too small so they took him to the doctor. They expressed their concerns to the doctor, who said to feed the little boy lots of toast.

The next morning, the wife gets up really early and makes a huge stack of toast. When the little boy comes down to breakfast, the mother says, "Take the top two slices. The rest are for your father."

A principal of a small middle school had a problem with a few older girls starting to use lipstick. When applying it in the bathroom they would then press their lips to the mirror and leave lip prints.

Before it got out of hand he thought of a way to stop it. He gathered all the girls together that wore lipstick and told them he wanted to meet with them in the ladies room that afternoon. They gathered in the restroom and found the principal and the school custodian waiting for them.

The principal explained that it was becoming a problem for the custodian to clean the mirror every night. He said he felt the ladies did not fully understand just how much of a problem it was and he wanted them to witness just how hard it was to clean.

The custodian then demonstrated. He took a long brush on a handle out of a box. He then dipped the brush in the nearest toilet, moved to the mirror and proceeded to remove the lipstick.

That was the last day the girls pressed their lips on the mirror.

Tompkins Nails has a new line of nails that they wish to sell.

They hire a big shot advertising agency. One salesman begins work on the advertising campaign to sell the new nails.

After a month the salesman calls a meeting with the board of directors from Tompkins, so he can show them what he has come up with. The salesman pulls away the covers revealing a poster of Jesus Christ nailed to a cross, and across the bottom in big letters: "We Used Tompkins Nails".

Not many of the directors were particularly impressed with this, and they thought that they had too many religious builders in the local trade who would be rather upset by this poster. They tell the salesman he has another month to come up with something better.

A month later, the board of directors reconvene. The salesman is back with a new covered poster. After everyone is seated, the salesman rips the cover away to show a new poster. This time, it shows Jesus running away from the cross. The caption says, "We SHOULD Have Used Tompkins Nails!"

Always a fun joke to tell at Easter . . . keeps those "hate mail files" full.

"So how do i get myself off?"

Missy with AOL
so how do i get myself off?

There's various ways:

(1) I understand the best method is to have someone that you care for help with the task. Granted, that's not "getting yourself off," but it goes along with your general laziness -- someone else is doing all of the work for your gratification.

(2) Try doing it by hand. It's more satisfying, but you have to know what you're doing or you're liable to go blind.

*(3) Use a machine. I'd say that'd "beat your hand" but you're liable to get **completely** confused.*

out am i stupid?

but you know what. i have enjoyed argueing with you and i like you jokes. so don't stop my subcription. do you still want to talk to each other?

Yes, dear, you're still stupid.

That's NOT what you're supposed to do with what you forwarded me.

You're young enough to be my daughter so I'm afraid flirting and chatting with you is out of the question. What on earth would we talk about?

Ravi in Kuwait
PLEASE UNSUBSCRIBE ME AND TAKE ME OFF YOUR MAILING LIST. THANK YOU

I deleted the message and three minutes later I got this

PLEASE TAKE ME OFF YOUR LIST THANKS

After deleting that one, one minute later I got this:

PLEASE KEEP ME ON YOU LIST AND SEND JOKE A DAY THANKS

riacric with AOL
I'm an AOL captive until I have to start paying! I can't believe the level of stupidity of most of these people. I pray they aren't driving the same roads as me. Only you would believe the shit that gets into my mailbox. My kids are allowed to surf only if I'm sitting next to them; how can anybody complain about adult content getting to their kids when they aren't anywhere around? I have 2 sets of standards, what I like & what I want my kids exposed to. Personally, I never miss a day at your site, but I'd never let my kid shave access. I want them to stay smart! LOL! How did such tight-assed cretins find your site in the first place? I think you could retire if you charged complaining assholes$29.95 to lodge their beefs. Call it "Incompetent Asshole Fee" and send me 1% so we can both retire! People, unless you have a very talented 3' dick, do not indulge in a pissing contest with Ray!!! You're going to lose every time!

A three foot dick, huh? Well, only when I'm not aroused.

3' at rest? You're in the wrong business, my friend. Let me "market" you & we'll both make a bundle. Or at least **I'll** have a bundle of fun! Unsurpassed wit AND a Hmm-hmm; your ex must be a complete whacko or one of those AOL'ers who can't unsub!

Wizard with Netva
RAY, I HAVE TO WONDER WHAT YOUR CHILDHOOD AT HOME WAS LIKEWHEN YOU FIND IT NECESSARY TO BULLY

AND BELITTLE OTHERS AROUND. NOT ONLY DO I FIND YOU NOT SO SMART - YOUR APPEAR VERY UNLEARNEDIN THOSE THINGS THAT EITHER MAKE US HUMAN OR INHUMAN.

WIZARD

Diane:

My childhood was **wonderful**. *I had two parents that loved me and in return I absolutely adored them. I was never "abused," "humiliated," or "made fun of." They encouraged me to learn, though my father never finished high school and my mom never spent a day in school beyond the 12th grade.*

One of the things that took me a loooong time to learn, tho, was to quit dealing with stupidity. In any shape or form. Life is **way** *too short to have to put up with people who are just plain* **stupid**. *I won't do it anymore.*

In addition, I also don't abide people who want to deride me for what I do: attempt to bring a smile to people's faces every day. If someone wants to get nasty with me, they'll find a more than worthy opponent when they take me on. If you or anyone else DOESN'T like what I'm doing here, then exercise your God-given ability to GO SOMEWHERE ELSE. Otherwise, you become a target and I **will** *take aim at you.*

You obviously don't find me "so smart" because you know you wouldn't come out on top in a verbal jousting match between the two of us, either. So, you resort to personal insults.

Finally, I'm pretty learned in the things that make me "human." I'll gladly turn to you when I need to learn how to be an "inhuman."

Ray
Joke A Day

THERE IS AN OLD JOKE THAT GOES: TWO CARS MEET IN THE MIDDLE OF ABRIDGE, ONE GUY STICKS HIS HEAD OUT THE WINDOW AND YELLS "I DON'TBACK UP FOR FOOLS!" THE OTHER GUY SAYS "WELL I DO," AND HE BACKSOFF THE BRIDGE. I DON'T NEED TO PROVE MYSELF BY GETTING

IN TO AVERBAL OR VIRTUAL WORDAGE MATCH WITH YOU.
I KNOW WHO ANDWHAT I AM AND WHAT I DO AND DON'T
STAND FOR. I DON'T NEED CENTRESTAGE - I'LL BACK OFF
THE BRIDGE.

*Make sure you back straight up. Although, on the other hand, it'd be
funny as hell to watch to you back right off the bridge into the river . . .*

"It was time for Father John's Saturday night bath . . ."

It was time for Father John's Saturday night bath, and the young nun, Sister Magdalene, had prepared the bath water and towels just the way the old nun had instructed.

Sister Magdalene was also instructed not to look at Fr. John's nakedness if she could help it, do whatever he told her to do, and pray.

The next morning the old nun asked Sister Magdalene how the Saturday night bath had gone.

"Oh, Sister," said the young nun dreamily. "I've been saved."

"Saved? And how did that fine thing come about?" asked the old nun.

"Well, when Fr. John was soaking in the tub, he asked me to wash him, and while I was washing him he guided my hand down between his legs where he said the Lord keeps the Key to Heaven."

"Did he now?" said the old nun evenly.

Sister Magdalene continued, "And Fr. John said that if the Key to Heaven fit my lock, the portals of Heaven would be opened to me and I would be assured of salvation and eternal peace. And then Father John guided his Key to Heaven into my lock."

"Is that a fact?" said the old nun even more evenly.

"At first it hurt terribly, but Fr. John said the pathway to salvation was often painful and that the glory of God would soon swell my heart with ecstasy. And it did; it felt so good being saved."

"That wicked old Devil!" said the old nun. "He told me it was Gabriel's Horn, and I've been blowing it for 40 years!"

"Johnny, where's your homework?" Miss Martin said sternly to the little boy while holding out her hand.

"My dog ate it," was his solemn response.

"Johnny, I've been a teacher for eighteen years. Do you really expect me to believe that?"

"It's true, Miss Martin, I swear," insisted Johnny. "I had to force him, but he ate it!"

There is a little Mercedes 280 SL in Toronto being driven by a gorgeous blonde, and the plate reads: WAS HIS

Remember my comments about lawyers a while ago? Things keep going the way they're going and my ex can put that label on this book.

This was on a Guns & Roses tape -- but I don't think it's what Tipper Gore had in mind:

"This album contains language which some listeners may find objectionable. They can FUCK OFF and buy something from the New Age section."

A few nights ago a few friends and I were in a bar, telling all the Polish jokes we knew; boy what a feast! Anyway, I ducked into the restroom to sprinkle the old porcelain. While I was in there, this big guy came in and said to me, "Hey pal, I'm Polish and I don't like you telling all those Polish jokes!"

So I said, "Well, they're not against you, pal, just against anyone in Poland."

"My mother is in Poland!" he screamed, and pulled out a razor.

Boy, was I scared! I was sure he would have killed me if he had found a place to plug it in!

At a pharmacy, a blonde asked to use the infant scale to weigh the baby she held in her arms. The clerk explained that the device was out for repairs, but said that she would figure the infant's weight by weighing the woman and baby together on the adult scale, then weighing the mother alone and subtracting the second amount from the first.

"It won't work," countered the woman. "I'm not the mother, I'm the aunt."

Wife to husband: "I'll let you explain to your son why his sister can have training bras but he can't have training condoms."

A man in a bar with his Labrador at his feet was intrigued to see another dog owner enter the bar. "That's a strange looking dog you have there," he said.

"Yes, he is, rather," said the newcomer, "but he's a great fighter."

"Is he, now? I bet he isn't as good a fighter as my Fang here."

"All right -- how much do you wanna bet?"

"Ten dollars."

"You're on."

So the two men let their dogs fight. Eventually the Labrador crawled, battered and bloody, to his master's side.

"I'd never thought I'd see Fang get defeated," said the loser's master, handing over the ten dollars, "especially by such an odd-looking one like yours."

"Yes, he does look a little peculiar," agreed the winner's master. "But he looked even odder before I shaved his mane off . . ."

God offered his tablet of commandments to the world. He first approached the Italians. "What commandments do you offer?" they asked. He answered, "Thou shalt not murder." They answered, "Sorry, we are not interested."

Next, He offered it to the Romanians. "What commandments do you offer?" they asked. He answered, "Thou shalt not steal." They answered, "Sorry, we are not interested."

Next, He offered them to the French. "What commandments do you offer?" they asked. "Thou shalt not covet thy neighbor's wife." "Sorry, we are not interested," they answered.

Finally, He approached the Jews. "How much?" they asked. "It's free," He answered. "We'll take ten of them!"

The tourist had lost his way on a back road and stopped at the farmhouse to ask if he could be put up for the night. "Well, we're a mite crowded, since there's already someone in the spare room," replied the farmer. "But I guess you can stay if you don't mind sharing the bed with a red-haired schoolteacher."

"Look," said the tourist, "I want you to know I'm a gentleman."

"Well," mused the farmer, "as far as I can tell, so is the red-haired schoolteacher."

A young Jewish boy starts attending public school in a small town. The teacher of the one-room school decides to use her position to try to influence the new student. She asks the class, "Who was the greatest man that ever lived?"

A girl raises her hand and says, "I think George Washington was the greatest man that ever lived because he is the Father of our country." The teacher replies, "Well, that's a good answer, but that's not the answer I am looking for."

Another young student raises his hand and says, "I think Abraham Lincoln was the greatest man that lived because he freed the slaves and helped end the Civil War."

"Well, that's another good answer, but that is not the one I was looking for."

Then the new Jewish boy raises his hand and says, "I think Jesus Christ was the greatest man that ever lived."

The teacher's mouth drops open in astonishment. "Yes!" she says, "that's the answer I was looking for." She then brings him up to the front of the classroom and gives him a lollipop.

Later, during recess, another Jewish boy approaches him as he is licking his lollipop. He says, "Why did you say, 'Jesus Christ'?"

The boy stops licking his lollipop and replies, "I know it's Moses, and YOU know it's Moses, but business is business."

A blonde went to the appliance store sale and found a bargain.

"I would like to buy this TV," she told the salesman. "Sorry, we don't sell to blondes," he replied.

She hurried home and dyed her hair, then came back and again told the salesman, "I would like to buy this TV."

"Sorry, we don't sell to blondes," he replied.

"Darn, he recognized me," she thought. She went for a complete disguise this time, haircut and new color, new outfit, big sunglasses, then waited a few days before she again approached the salesman. "I would like to buy this TV."

"Sorry, we don't sell to blondes," he replied.

Frustrated, she exclaimed, "How do you know I'm a blonde?"

"Because that's a microwave," he replied.

A doctor and his wife were having an argument at breakfast. "You aren't so good in bed either!" the doctor shouted and stormed out of the door off to work. By midmorning he decided that he would try to make amends and called home. After many rings his wife finally picked up the phone.

"What took you so long to answer?"

"I was in bed."

"What were you doing in bed this late?"

"I was getting a second opinion."

Jon bought two horses and could never remember which was which. A neighbor suggested that he cut the tail of one horse and that worked great until the other horse got his tail caught in a bush. It tore just right and looked exactly like the other horse's tail and our friend was stuck again.

The neighbor suggested Jon notch the ear of one horse. That worked fine until the other horse caught his ear on a barbed wire fence. Once again our friend couldn't tell them apart.

The neighbor suggested he measure the horses for height. When he did, he was very pleased to find that the white horse was 2 inches taller than the black.

There is a report of a 2 seater private plane which crashed into a large cemetery in Poland.

The Polish Fire Dept. has reported recovering over 300 bodies and is still digging . . .

Women don't care how big your dick is. They would, but they're too busy worrying about the size of their tits.

An old woman in the West Virginia hills received a letter from her grandniece, who'd gone off to the big city to seek her fortune. Puzzled by the writing and the contents, she read to her husband, "Judi says here that she's got herself a job in a . . . a . . . a . . . well, it must be a *message* parlor."

"I reckon city folks must leave word there fer their neighbors and kinfolk. Them not having back fences and all," her husband said. "Does Judi say how much they's a payin' her?"

"Well, that's the part I can't make out. For the life of me, Paw, she says she gets some $35 for a hand delivered message and $60 if she *blows* it to them!"

A cowboy walked into a barbershop, sat on the barber's chair, and said, "I'll have a shave and a shoe shine." The barber began to lather his face while a woman with the biggest, firmest, most beautiful breasts that he had ever seen knelt down and began to shine his shoes.

The cowboy said, "Young lady, you and I should go and spend some time in a hotel room."

She replied, "I'm married and my husband wouldn't like that."

The cowboy said, "Tell him you're working overtime and I'll pay you the difference."

She said, "You tell him. He is the one shaving you."

"And will there be anything else, sir?" the bellboy asked after setting out an elaborate dinner for two.

"No, thank you," the gentleman replied. "That will be all."

As the young man turned to leave, he noticed a beautiful satin negligee on the bed. "Anything for your wife?" he asked.

"Yeah! That's a good idea," the fellow said. "Please bring up a postcard."

With the help of a fertility specialist, a 65-year-old woman has a baby. All her relatives come to visit and meet the newest member of their family.

When they ask to see the baby, the 65-year-old mother says "Not yet." A little later they ask to see the baby again. Again the mother says "Not yet."

Finally they say, "When can we see the baby?" And the mother says, "When the baby cries." And they ask, "Why do we have to wait until the baby cries?"

The new mother says, "Because I forgot where I put it."

A waiter brings the customer the steak he ordered with his thumb over the meat.

"Are you crazy?" yelled the customer. "You've got your thumb on my steak!"

"What?" answers the waiter, "you want it to fall on the floor again?"

A guy is standing at a urinal when he notices that a midget is watching him. Although the little fellow is staring at him intently, the guy doesn't get uncomfortable until the midget drags a small stepladder up next to him, climbs it, and proceeds to admire his privates at close range.

"Wow," comments the midget, "Those are the nicest balls I have ever seen!"

Surprised and flattered the man thanks the midget and starts to move away.

"Listen, I know this is a rather strange request," says the little fellow, "but I wonder if you would mind if I touched them."

Again the man is rather startled, but seeing no real harm in it, he obliges the request. The midget reaches out, gets a tight grip on the man's balls, and says, "OK, hand me your wallet or I'll jump off the ladder!"

Two kids were having the standard argument about whose father could beat up whose father.

One boy said, "My father is better than your father."

The other kid said, "Well, my mother is better than your mother."

The first boy paused, "I guess you're right. My father says the same thing."

One day a 5th grade class was taking a field trip but the weather was extremely bad and the trip was to be delayed and they had to stay in a motel for the night. So little Johnny was sleeping in the same room as his teacher.

In the middle of the night the teacher woke up and was frightened by the sight of Johnny standing right over her. He asked if he could sleep with her because he couldn't sleep. She said OK, then Johnny asked to lie a little closer and she said OK. Then he asked if he could put his finger in her belly button, and she said, "NO."

"But my Mommy lets me do it when I can't sleep and it helps."

So the teacher says, "OK, fine, do whatever your mom lets you do."

And a few minutes later the teacher says, "OH, *that's* not my belly button."

And Johnny says, "That's not my finger."

A farmer goes to confession for the first time in twenty years and tells the priest he's been having sexual intercourse with a pig ever since his wife died.

The priest asks him if he intends to continue doing it and whether the pig is a male or female.

"No! I'm not doing it anymore!" says the farmer. "And the pig is a female, of course. What the hell do you think I am -- a goddamn queer?"

There was a farmer who had a brown cow and a white cow and he wanted to breed them, so borrowed his neighbor's bull and turned it loose in the pasture. He told his son to watch for the bull to finish, then come in tell him.

"Yeah, Daddy, yeah!" said the little boy.

After a while the boy came into the living where his father was talking with some friends. "Hey, Daddy," said the boy.

"Yes," replied his father.

"The bull just fucked the brown cow."

There was a sudden lull in the conversation. The father said "Excuse me," and took his son outside. "Son, you mustn't use language like that in front of company. You should say, 'The bull surprised the brown cow.' Now go and watch and tell me when the bull surprises the white cow."

The father went back inside the house. After a while the boy came in and said, "Hey, Daddy!"

"Yes, son? Did the bull surprise the white cow?"

"He sure did, Daddy! He fucked the brown cow again!"

A little girl asked her mother, "Can I go outside and play with the boys?"

Her mother replied, "No, you can't play with the boys, they're too rough."

The little girl thought about it for a few moments and asked, "If I can find a smooth one, can I play with him?"

"I find it very sad that you use your site to make fun of people with inferior intelligence."

Joyce with optidynamic

While I enjoy your list and I read it everyday, I find it very sad that you use your site to make fun of people with inferior intelligence. Though some of the exchanges may be humorous, think of how the people being made fun of must feel. Though typos and incorrect grammer are easy to come by and easy to overlook, I really don't think that they are any indication of someone's education level. It is very easy to misspell words and make other similar mistakes without realizing it. Though I usually agree with your opinions of the people, I think it is cruel to take their letters and mistakes public. After all, everyone makes mistakes, including you and myself.

*Well, who **else** am I going to make fun of except those with inferior intelligence? Those rocket scientists and brain surgeons are **tough** to insult.*

Martha with gateway

Dear Ray,

I loved the April Fool's Trick this year. That has led to an unfortunate problem. Now, I am TRULY, deeply, madly lustful for you! I wish I could meet you, but I guess I'll have to be content with just receiving you JAD e-mails.... Sniff, sniff!

Love ya!,

Martha

Dcrowe with AOL

I have told your several times to stop sending me jokes. Do I have to sue you before you stop sending them?
James T. S . . ., Attorney at Law

Well, Counselor, it'll be an interesting case.

"Your honor, I'm suing Joke A Day because they wouldn't stop sending me jokes."

"Counselor, did you sign up for the list?"

"Uhh, yes, your honor . . ."

"Did you receive the welcome letter with the instructions on how to get off the list?"

"Uhh, yes, your honor . . ."

"Did you receive documentation with EVERY joke sent out on how to remove yourself from the list?"

"Uh, yes, your honor . . ."

"Was knowing how to READ and FOLLOW DIRECTIONS necessary in Law School, Counselor?

"Uh, yes, your honor . . ."

"Then, Counselor, why is it you can't read and follow the directions to get off the list? You followed them to get ON the list, didn't you?"

"Uh, yes, your honor . . ."

"Then I rule you're an idiot. Next case."

Diane with webtv
Dear Ray,

You have made me laugh for the first time in months. Recently, both my Mother and Father have passed away and I thought I'd never laugh again. The Judi awards were hilarious. Keep up the good work and again thank you.

Diane

P.S. I was not going to send this message after your reference to your "tirades about AOL and WebTV," but I figured what the hell? Once again, a million thanks for bringing me out of the darkness for a little while.

Sorry to hear about your folks. My dad passed away 4 years ago last month and there's not a single day goes by I don't think about him.

I'm glad I could bring a little sunshine into your life. Makes all those Judis and Dweebs worth it.

"*A farmer is arrested and accused of bestiality*"

A farmer is arrested and accused of bestiality. Too indigent to hire an attorney, the farmer is visited by the Public Defender.

"So," the farmer says, "are you any good?"

The Public Defender responds, "Well, I'm not so good at opening arguments, and I'm not so good at summations, and, well I'm not so good at anything in between."

The farmer responds incredulously, "So what are you good at?"

The attorney responds, "Well, I'm pretty good at picking juries."

The farmer, not having an alternative, throws his fate to the Public Defender.

The day of the trial arrives, and the farmer is being grilled by the Prosecuting Attorney.

"So, Mr. Farmer, isn't it true that the goat in question is your goat?"

"Yep, she is."

"And, Mr. Farmer, isn't it true that on the day in question you were seen out in the field having sex with your goat?"

There is silence in the courtroom, and before the farmer can answer, over in the jury box, one juror leans over to another and whispers, "You know, a good goat will do that."

Dad came home one day in an exceptionally horny mood and took his wife upstairs for sex. Just when they were really getting into it, their young son entered the room and started to cry.

"What's wrong, son?" the father asked. "Why are you crying?"

"You're hurting my mommy," the little boy replied.

"No, no," the father reassured. "I'm not hurting her. We are making babies."

This seemed to calm the boy, and when he left the room the couple went back to their business.

The next day the father came home from work and found his son on the steps, crying.

"What's the matter NOW?" asked Dad.

"It's those babies you were making with mommy yesterday," the boy answered. "The mailman is upstairs eating them."

Three boys are in the schoolyard bragging on how great their fathers are.

The first one says, "Well, my father runs the fastest. He can fire an arrow, and start to run, I tell you, he gets there before the arrow."

The second one says: "Ha! You think that's fast! My father is a hunter. He can shoot his gun and be there before the bullet."

The third one listens to the other two and shakes his head. He then says: "You two know nothing about fast. My father is a civil servant. He stops working at 4:30 and he is home by 3:45!!"

A Scoutmaster was teaching his Boy Scouts about survival in the desert.

"What are the three most important things you should have with you in case you get lost in the desert?" he asked. Several hands went up, and many important things were suggested such as food, matches, etc.

Then one little boy in the back eagerly raised his hand. "Yes, Timmy, what are the three most important things you would bring with you?" asked the Scoutmaster.

Timmy replied: "A compass, a canteen of water, and a deck of cards."

"Why's that, Timmy?"

"Well," answered Timmy, "the compass is to find the right direction, the water is to prevent dehydration."

"And what about the deck of cards?" asked the Scoutmaster.

"Well, Sir, as soon as you start playing Solitaire, someone is bound to come up behind you and say, 'Put that red nine on top of that black ten!'"

Q. What should you do if your girlfriend starts smoking?
A. Slow down and use a lubricant.

Q. Why do women pay more attention to their appearance than to improving their minds?
A. Because most men are stupid, but few are blind.

A woman goes to her doctor, complaining that her husband is 300% impotent. The doctor says, "I'm not sure I understand what you mean."

She says, "Well, the first 100% you can imagine. In addition, he burned his tongue and broke his finger!"

Lori, the pert and pretty nurse, took her troubles to a resident psychiatrist in the hospital where she worked.

"Doctor, you must help me," she pleaded. "It's gotten so that every time I date one of the young doctors here, I end up in bed with him. And then afterward, I feel guilty and depressed for a week."

"I see." nodded the psychiatrist. "And you, no doubt, want me to strengthen your will power and resolve in this matter."

"For God's sake, NO!!!" exclaimed the nurse. "I want you to fix it so I won't feel guilty and depressed afterward."

There were two guys on a motorcycle driving down the road. The driver was wearing a leather jacket that didn't have a zipper or any buttons.

Finally he stopped the bike and told the other guy, "I can't drive any longer with the air hitting me in my chest."

After thinking for a while he decided to put the coat on backwards to block the air from hitting him. They were driving down the road and came around this curb and wrecked. The farmer that lived there called the police and told them what happened.

The police asked him, "Are either of them showing any life signs?"

The farmer then said, "Well, that first one was 'til I turned his head around the right way."

A couple returned from their honeymoon and it's obvious to everyone that they are not talking to each other. The groom's best man takes him aside and asks what is wrong.

"Well," replied the man "when we had finished making love on the first night, as I got up to go to the bathroom I put a $50 bill on the pillow without thinking."

"Oh, you shouldn't worry about that too much," said his friend. "I'm sure your wife will get over it soon enough -- she can't expect you to have been saving yourself all these years!"

The groom nodded gently and said, "I don't know if I can get over this though. She gave me $20 change!"

In front of a delicatessen, an art connoisseur noticed a mangy little kitten lapping up milk from a saucer. The saucer, he realized with a start, was a rare and precious piece of pottery.

He strolled into the store and offered two dollars for the cat. "It's not for sale," said the proprietor.

"Look," said the collector, "that cat is dirty and undesirable, but I'm eccentric. I like cats that way. I'll raise my offer to ten dollars."

"It's a deal," said the proprietor, and pocketed the ten on the spot.

"For that sum I'm sure you won't mind throwing in the saucer," said the connoisseur. "The kitten seems so happy drinking from it."

"Nothing doing," said the proprietor firmly. "That's my lucky saucer. From that saucer, so far this week I've sold 34 cats."

Women do not snore, burp, sweat, or fart.
Therefore, they must "bitch" or they will blow up.

A hotel busboy looks through the keyhole of a honeymoon suite and says, "Wowie!"

A maid hears him, and pushes him out of the way for a look. She says, "Oh, my God!"

Just then the maitre d' is walking down the hall, and has her get out of the way so he can have a look. He takes a look and says, "I can't believe he complained about a hair in his soup last night."

A little old lady's phone rings late one night and she answers it.

"Hello," a deep voice on the other end says, "I know you. You'd like me to push you down on the bed and rip all your clothes off, lick your body all over and make rough love to you."

The old lady looks at the phone, blushing in amazement, and replies, "You can tell all this from a single 'Hello?'"

A man who lived in a block of apartments thought it was raining and put his head out the window to check. As he did so a glass eye fell into his hand.

He looked up to see where it came from in time to see a young woman looking down.

"Is this yours?" he asked.

She said, "Yes, could you bring it up?" and the man agreed.

On arrival she was profuse in her thanks and offered the man a drink. As she was very attractive he agreed. Shortly afterwards, she said, "I'm about to have dinner. There's plenty; would you like to join me?"

He readily accepted her offer and both enjoyed a lovely meal. As the evening was drawing to a close the lady said, "I've had a marvelous evening. Would you like to stay the night?"

The man hesitated then said, "Do you act like this with every man you meet?"

"No," she replied, "Only those who catch my eye."

In the high school gym, all the girls in the class were lined up against one wall, and all the boys against the opposite wall. Then, every ten seconds, they walked toward each other until they were half the previous distance apart. A mathematician, a physicist, and an engineer were asked, "When will the girls and boys meet?"

The mathematician said: "Never."

The physicist said: "In an infinite amount of time."

The engineer said: "Well, in about two minutes, they'll be close enough for all practical purposes."

A preacher retired and moved to the country to enjoy life and practice his hobby of yard work. Needing a lawn mower, he headed into town to buy one. On the way he saw a sign advertising a lawn mower for sale. He stopped at the house and a young lad came out to greet him. The preacher asked about the lawn mower and the kid said it was behind the house. The two went to look at the lawn mower. The engine was sputtering along at idle speed. The preacher increased the speed of the engine and mowed a few strips. Satisfied that the mower would do the job they settled on a price of $25.00.

Later in the day, the young lad was riding his bicycle when he spied the preacher pulling on the engine starter rope. The kid stopped and watched for a couple of minutes. He asked, "What's wrong?"

The reply came, "I can't get this mower started. Do you know how?"

The kid said, "Yep."

"Well, how do you do it? Tell me!" the preacher yelled.

The kid replied, "You have to cuss it."

The preacher rose up indignantly. "Now you listen here. I am a preacher and if I ever did cuss, not saying I have, I've forgotten how to do it after all these years."

With a wise look on his face well beyond his years, the kid said, "Preacher, you keep on pulling that rope and it'll all come back to ya."

A man comes home with his daughter, whom he has just taken to work. The little girl asks, "I saw you in your office with your secretary. Why do you call her a doll?"

Feeling his wife's gaze upon him, the man explains, "Well, Honey, my secretary is a very hard-working girl. She types like you wouldn't believe, she knows the computer system, and is very efficient."

"Oh. I thought it was because she closed her eyes when you lay her down on the couch."

Sue and Sally meet at their 30th class reunion, and they haven't seen each other since graduation. They begin to talk and bring each other up to date. The conversation covers their husbands, their children, homes, etc. and finally gets around to their sex lives.

Sue says, "It's OK. We get it on every week or so but it's no big adventure; how's yours?"

Sally replies "It's just great, ever since we got into S&M."

Sue is aghast. "Really, Sally, I never would have guessed that you would go for that."

"Oh, sure," says Sally, "He snores while I masturbate."

A magician was on stage doing his act, when he called for a volunteer from the audience. A man volunteered and went up on stage. The magician told him to pick up the 16 lb. sledgehammer that was on stage next to a cement block and break the block apart with the sledgehammer, so the audience would know the sledgehammer was real.

So, the man swung the sledgehammer with all his might and shattered the cement block. The magician now told the man to hit him square in the face with the sledgehammer. Horrified, the man said, "No way. It'll probably kill you." The magician insisted that the man hit him in the face, saying, "I'll be fine. I promise you -- go ahead." "Well," the man replied, "OK, here goes."

Again, the man swung the sledgehammer and aimed it at the magician's face. The result was very bloody. The magician's nose was crushed, teeth fell out, blood everywhere. He went into a coma for the next six months and was confined to a hospital.

The man who swung the sledgehammer felt very guilty and visited the magician in the hospital every day while the magician was in his coma.

One day, about six months later, one of the magician's eyes opened, and his fingers flexed a bit. A moment later, the other eye opened. After a few more moments, the magician sat straight up and said, "Ta-da!"

A guy went into a bar and subsequently met a nice girl. They had a few drinks and wound up at his place, in bed.

They were having a great time. While she was on top, she suddenly had an epileptic seizure. She was foaming at the mouth and shaking. The clueless man thought it was great -- best sex he'd ever had.

He finished, but she was still shaking and thrashing about with her seizure. He began to get worried. He drove her to the emergency room.

A nurse asked what the problem was and he replied, "I think her orgasm's stuck!"

A juggler, driving to his next performance, is stopped by the police. "What are these matches and lighter fluid doing in your car?" asks the cop.

"I'm a juggler and I juggle flaming torches in my act."

"Oh yeah?" says the doubtful cop. "Let's see you do it." The juggler gets out and starts juggling the blazing torches masterfully.

A couple driving by slows down to watch. "Wow," says the driver to his wife. "I'm glad I quit drinking. Look at the test they're giving now!"

I was just visiting some friends who have a real working farm. I was watching this one rooster chasing after this hen, when the friend's wife came out to feed them. The rooster stopped chasing the hen at once and ran over to begin eating. I stood there thinking to myself, "Damn! I hope I never get that hungry."

"Could you please explain it without your typical sarcasm and mocking?"

Celina with ATT
Hmmmm..........I didn't really get the joke on Friday about the mute guys in a golf cart. Could you please explain it without your typical sarcasm and mocking?

No, I can't explain it without my typical saracasm and mocking.

Maybe at least you could learn to spell "sarcasm" right, then.

Maybe.

Then again, I understood the joke.

So did my 5th grader.

This was, inexplicably, in response to my Mother's Day Card I sent to everyone:

tbond4334 with AOL
dont be stupid. if you sent a joke i probababl;y got a chuckle. must have made a mistake. too much stupid e mail ya know? still. dont send me more. dumnass. and i mean it. reporting you to aol. youll be closed down! get it?

Closed down by AOL?

*Yeah, boy, AOL has the **finest** and most **intelligent** people on the whole Internet.*

im not a mother. single dad! dont have time for your garbage so tak me off you stupid list!!! get it ass?

Yeah, your letter pretty much proves you ARE a "mutha." Odds are, you more than likely didn't HAVE one though . . . or she'd have taught you some manners, dumbass.

by the by, i am a singlr dad. and i teach my girls manners. obviously you were not!!!! youve a lot to lesrn if you want to sell your product moron! i make 200000 a year. im good. your just stupid. get off the net cause yor a failure

Yeah, I have all kinds of manners. They don't extend to people like you who've got the brains God gave a groundhog.

*I have **no** trouble believing you make $2000.00 a year. That "Hooked on Phonics" course you stole from the Public Library paid off, huh? Maybe you can answer just how many tubes of "Ben Gay" a "Sanitation Engineer" goes through at the end of each shift. It's the question of the ages.*

I'm not selling any "product," TB. Is that what you're looking for online -- "product"? I personally think you should knock off using the stuff myself (you're not capable of making coherent sentences) but, to be helpful, for "product," point your browser (yeah, I know I'm talking to an even dumber than usual AOL member) towards www.drugdealer.com They'll hook you up.

Dan with home
Ray, I've just read the dweeb letters. You are an arrogant, insensitive, snide, condescending, sarcastic asshole with a superiority complex. I must say, I love it. I also fit that description, and I think it's damn funny the way you stick to these morons every day. I just don't know how you do it day in and day out. Back in the days when I had an AOL account (forgive me, I was young and didn't know any better) I used to love taking on a wayward moron and making them look even dumber, but I ran out of energy for it after a while. Your ability to trounce the idiots of the world day after day is truly admirable. From one sarcastic asshole to another, keep up the good work.

Flygirl with AOL
please stop my email as i am too busty to read them.

There's a minimum requirement of 38D for me to unsubscribe you.

*Send me a picture of how busty you are. We **may** have to conduct personal, on-site, open-shirt, hands-on inspections, by the way, to verify that you've met the requirements. In some cases, there's an oral exam.*

Jayant with hotmail
This joke was pretty funny except for one problem. When you inferred that in Amanpreet's country there were 79 ways to make love, you must have been talking about the Kama Sutra. The one critical mistake, which makes the joke sound kind of dumb, is that the Kama Sutra is a Hindu scripture and Allah is the God in Islam.

Oops...it just makes the joke teller look stupid and we wouldnt want that.

Well, there's just one problem with your analysis:

It's so completely stupid as to be unbelievable.

*Who mentioned Kama Sutra? Who mentioned Hindu? Who mentioned Allah? No one. There was no specific county implied. It was (dare I say it?) a **joke**.*

But, since you've taken such umbrage at this joke, why not dissect the following one for me? (I've been saving it for just such an event):

Amanpreet died and was sent on up to heaven. As he approached the pearly gates, Saint Peter approached him to welcome him in. Amanpreet politely told him "Thank you very much, Saint Peter. As you may be aware, I am a Muslim, and would really appreciate being greeted by Muhammad."

Saint Peter replied, "Certainly, if that's your wish. Take the staircase on your left and go up."

Approaching the top of the staircase, Amanpreet was met by Buddha, waiting to welcome him into Heaven. Once again Amanpreet explained to him that he was a Muslim and wanted to be greeted by Muhammad. Buddha directed him up another staircase, where this time he was met by Moses.

Amanpreet, slightly exasperated, offered his thanks to Moses and a little more vehemently, asked that he be greeted by Muhammad. Moses pointed to a golden escalator, and told him to take it up to the top floor where he would find Muhammad.

Arriving at the top floor, Amanpreet found himself being led to a table, where this time, Jesus himself was waiting to greet him. Amanpreet was angry by now, and had had enough. "Thank you very much, Jesus. I mean no offense to you or anyone else, but I AM A MUSLIM, AND I DEMAND TO SEE THE GREAT PROPHET MUHAMMED!!!"

"You want to see Muhammad?" asked Jesus with a puzzled expression.

"YES! Very much so!" replied Amanpreet.

"OK. Fine. No problem." replied Jesus. "By the way, how do you take your coffee?"

This time it was Amanpreet who was puzzled. "Uh, black, no sugar. Why?"

Jesus stands up from the table and snaps his fingers. "YO! MUHAMMED! Over here. Two coffees. Black. No Sugar."

ladylove with AOL
the same joke has been on for the past 3 days. Why??

Because we don't update the website on weekends. We've never updated the website on weekends.

Geez~~ are you too lazy on weekends to put an new joke on?? It does say "jokeaday" NOT "samejokefor3days" You can remove me from your list........there are plenty out there that dont have bad attitudes like you.

Why don't all of you people on AOL just stay away from the Internet? It's too complicated for you folks out here. You don't seem to be able to grasp real simple concepts.

I don't unsubscribe anyone. Especially clueless AOL people.

sorry accidently deleted....could you resend

You're the first person in the history of Joke A Day to ever ask to have a flame resent . . . don't you get enough abuse by the sheer fact that you're an AOL user? You have to have it repeated?

DYRT with AOL

Hi!

Here's my story. I'm sure it's not new, but it reinforces you dislike for AOL (A##hole's On Line).

I'm not new to Joke a Day. I subscribed through Internet Explorer at my place of work. I'm not crazy about AOL either, but "Hubby" wanted to use AOL. I'm not "internet illiterate," but he is very much so. I've always heard that if you are stupid, you pick AOL. Here's the kicker - He wanted AOL so much, that we had to change our telephone local calling area so that we would not be charged by the minute for making a non-local call. Our base bill went from $16 per month to $45 (I'm also making him pay for that in addition to the AOL monthly fee). We could have gotten the same thing through a local provider for just the monthly fee, which is less expensive than AOL's and still have 24 hour tech support and good response time. I keep telling myself it takes all types to make the world go'round.

Hon, you've missed the most obvious solution. It's time to get a new husband. :) Look, everyone is upgrading, so now's the time to get one of those Y2K compliant hubbies.

"Upon arriving in Greece . . ."

Upon arriving in Greece, a couple decided not to see the country the traditional touristy way but to hire a guide from one of the small villages. After finding a guide, he took them on a boat ride showing them the sights of Greece.

After a while, they passed a grove of fig trees.

After the tourists commented on the beauty of the trees, the guide said, "See all those trees? I planted every one of those trees. I nurtured every one of those trees. But do they call me Zorba, the tree-planter? No."

The couple looked a little confused at his outrage but kept quiet. After about 15 minutes, they passed a nice village on the bank of the river. The tourists commented on the beauty of the village.

Again, the guide went off. "See all those houses? I built every one of those houses. With these two hands alone, I built those houses. But do they call me Zorba, the house-builder? NO."

The couple again looked confused and worried about the guide's outrage. They didn't want to annoy him again. After about 30 minutes, they passed a small fleet of fishing boats. The husband commented on the boats.

"You see all those boats? I built those boats. With these two hands, I built every boat and not a one has sunk. But do they call me Zorba, the boat-builder? NO!!"

The tourists stayed quiet until they saw something which the guide could not have built. "Look at those lovely donkeys," said the wife.

The guide looked at them and said, "Oh, but you fuck one donkey..."

The new nun goes to her first confession. She tells the priest that she has a terrible secret and he tells her that her secret is safe in the sanctity of the confessional.

She says, "Father, I never wear panties under my habit."

The priest chuckles and says, "That's not so serious. Say five Hail Marys, five Our Fathers and do six cartwheels on your way to the altar."

The Michaels family owned a small farm in Canada, just yards away from the North Dakota border. Their land had been the subject of a minor dispute between the United States and Canada for generations. Mrs. Michaels, who had just celebrated her ninetieth birthday, lived on the farm with her son and three grandchildren.

One day, her son came into her room holding a letter. "I just got some news, Mom," he said. "The government has come to an agreement with the people in Washington. They've decided that our land is really part of the United States. We have the right to approve or disapprove of the agreement. What do you think?"

"What do I think?" his mother said. "Jump at it! Call them right now and tell them we accept! I don't think I could stand another one of those Canadian winters!"

Two confirmed bachelors sat talking. Their conversation drifted from politics to cooking. "I got a cookbook once," said the first, "but I could never do anything with it."

"Too much fancy cooking in it, eh?" asked the second.

"You said it. Every one of the recipes began the same way -- 'Take a clean dish and . . .'"

The wife chewed out her husband at the company picnic a while back. "Doesn't it embarrass you that people have seen you go up to the buffet table five times?"

"Not a bit," the husband replied. "I just tell them I'm filling up the plate for you!"

One day in the Garden of Eden, Eve calls out to God, "Lord, I have a problem!"

"What's the problem, Eve?"

"Lord, I know you've created me and have provided this beautiful garden and all of these wonderful animals, and that hilarious comedy snake, but I'm just not happy."

"Why is that, Eve?" came the reply from above.

"Lord, I am lonely. And I'm sick to death of apples."

"Well, Eve, in that case, I have a solution. I shall create a man for you."

"What's a 'man', Lord?"

"This man will be a flawed creature, with aggressive tendencies, an enormous ego and an inability to empathize or listen to you properly. All in all, he'll give you a hard time. But, he'll be bigger and faster and more muscular than you. He'll be really good at fighting and kicking a ball about and hunting fleet-footed ruminants, and not altogether bad in the sack."

"Sounds great," says Eve, with an ironically raised eyebrow.

"Yeah, well. He's better than a poke in the eye with a burnt stick. But, you can have him on one condition."

"What's that, Lord?"

"You'll have to let him believe that I made him first."

"In screwing a ewe," the old mountain man was explaining to the horny young shepherd, "you sneak up behind her, quietly loosen your bootlaces, and then grab her rear legs and jam them into your boots."

"But that's awkward," objected the horny one. "In that position, how can I kiss her?"

I heard from the Animal Rights activists over this one again. I dunno, did the shepherd have bad breath or something?

The strong young man at the construction site was bragging that he could outdo anyone in a feat of strength. He made a special case of making fun of one of the older workmen. After several minutes, the older worker had had enough.

"Why don't you put your money where your mouth is," he said. "I will bet a week's wages that I can haul something in a wheelbarrow over to that outbuilding that you won't be able to wheel back."

"You're on, old man," the braggart replied. "Let's see what you got."

The old man reached out and grabbed the wheelbarrow by the handles. Then, nodding to the young man, he said, "All right. Get in."

An attorney went into a bar for a martini and found himself beside a scruffy-looking drunk who kept mumbling and studying something in his hand. He leaned closer while the drunk held the tiny object up to the light, slurring, "Well, it looks like plastic." Then he rolled it between his fingers, adding, "But it feels like rubber."

Curious, the attorney asked, "What do you have there?"

The drunk replied, "I don't know, but it looks like plastic and feels like rubber."

The attorney responded, "Let me take a look."

So the drunk handed it over and the lawyer rolled it between his thumb and fingers, then examined it closely by sniffing and licking it. "Yeah, it does look like plastic and feel like rubber, has no significant smell or taste; I sure don't know what it is.   Where did you get it?"

The drunk replied, "Out of my nose."

A man visited a psychiatrist to talk about his dreams. "Every night," the man said, "I dream that these three hideous monsters are sitting on the edge of my bed, ready to attack me."

"Hmmm," said the doctor. "I feel sure I can cure you of this problem. But the treatment will cost you somewhere between twenty and thirty thousand dollars."

"Thirty thousand dollars!" the man gasped. "Never mind getting rid of the monsters, Doctor. I think I'll go home and try to make friends with them."

A young man goes to a doctor for a physical examination. When he gets into the room, the man strips for his exam. He has a dick the size of a little kid's little finger.

A nurse standing in the room sees his "Little Willie" and begins to laugh hysterically.

The young man gives her a stern look and says, "You shouldn't laugh; it's been swollen like that for two weeks now!"

A mother was reading a book about animals to her 3-year-old daughter:
Mother: "What does the cow say?"

Child: "Moooo!"

Mother: "Great! What does the cat say?"

Child: "Meow."

Mother: "Oh, you're so smart! What does the frog say?"

And this wide-eyed little three-year-old looked up at her mother and replied, "Bud."

Some tourists in the Chicago Museum of Natural History are marveling at the dinosaur bones. One of them asks the guard, "Can you tell me how old the dinosaur bones are?"

The guard replies, "They are 3 million, four years, and six months old."

"That's an awfully exact number," says the tourist. "How do you know their age so precisely?"

The guard answers, "Well, the dinosaur bones were three million years old when I started working here, and that was four and a half years ago."

The visiting church school supervisor asks little Johnny during Bible class who broke down the walls of Jericho. Little Johnny replies that he does not know, but it definitely was not him.

The supervisor, taken aback by this lack of basic Bible knowledge, goes to the school principal and relates the whole incident.

The principal replies that he knows little Johnny, as well as his whole family, very well and can vouch for them. If little Johnny said that he did not do it, he as principal is satisfied that it is the truth.

Even more appalled, the supervisor goes to the regional Head of Education and relates the whole story.

After listening he replies: "I cannot see why you are making such a big issue out of this. We will get three quotes and fix the damned wall."

An old man woke up in the middle of the night and found, to his utter astonishment, that his pecker was as hard as a rock for the first time in two years.

He shook his wife by the shoulder until she woke up, and showed her his enormous boner.

"You see that thing, woman?" he happily exclaimed. "What do you think we ought to do with it?"

With one eye open, his wife replied, "Well, now that you've got all the wrinkles out, this might be a good time to wash it!"

When my husband and I arrived at an automobile dealership to pick up our car, we were told that the keys had been accidentally locked in it. We went to the service department and found a mechanic working feverishly to unlock the driver's side door.

As I watched from the passenger's side, I instinctively tried the door handle and discovered it was open. "Hey," I announced to the technician, "It's open!"

"I know," answered the young man. "I already got that side."

Fu, Bu and Chu immigrated to the USA from China. They decided to become American citizens, and "Americanize" their names.

Bu called himself "Buck"

Chu called himself "Chuck"

Fu decided to return to China.

One day when the teacher walked into the classroom, she noticed that someone had written the word 'PENIS' (in tiny letters) on the blackboard. She scanned the class looking for a guilty face. Finding none, she rubbed the word off and began class. The next day, the word 'PENIS' was written on the board again; this time it was written about halfway across the board. Again she looked around in vain for the culprit, so she proceeded with the day's lesson.

Every morning for about a week, she went into the classroom and found the same disgusting word written on the board, each day's being larger than the previous one, and each being rubbed off vigorously.

At the end of the second week, she walked in expecting to be greeted by the same word on the board but instead found the words: "The more you rub it, the bigger it gets."

The young Swedish au pair had been working for the Schmitts for more than a year. While hardworking and efficient, she still struggled with English. One day she told Mrs. Schmitt that she had received good news from her boyfriend Sven.

"He is coming visit me from army next week!"

"That's wonderful," the woman replied. "How long is his furlough?"

"Oh," the young woman said, "about long as Mr. Schmitt's. Maybe little thicker."

There was this group of four guys that were avid golfers and played every weekend. One week one of the four was unable to make it to the game. The guy that was unable to make it left a message at the clubhouse that said, "The tee time is set and you are going to play with my friend 'Bobby' so that you will still have your foursome."

The other three guys show up at the appointed tee time and were met by a beautiful woman who introduced herself as "Bobbie." The other three were a little wary about playing with a woman but since they didn't want to miss their tee time they went ahead and played.

After playing the front nine they were pretty loosened up around Bobbie especially after they found out that she could play. The foursome walks up to the par five eighteenth hole. Bobbie, who is shooting a respectable two over, makes two near perfect shots to get within 25ft of the hole.

She turns to the other three and says, "Guys, I think I know you well enough for this so I'll tell you. I am a scratch handicap golfer and I have never done better than three putt this hole. Whoever can help me make this putt and go even for the round, I'll take that person off to the No-Tell motel and we'll fuck like rabbits."

The first guy looks serious and says, " I think you should hit it left."

The second guy goes, "Nope, you should hit it right."

The third guy looks at Bobbie, sighs, walks over and picks up the ball and says, "Gee, guys, looks like a gimmee to me!"

Without a doubt, this joke wins hands down the title for "The One Everyone on AOL Didn't Understand." I swear, I must have received 200 letters asking me to explain the thing. Now that I think about it, every time I ever do a joke about golf, I get the same reaction. Maybe that's why golfers wear those stupid clothes -- it's the only laughs they can get.

A woman from (a small, impoverished, third world country of your choice) newly arrived in America discovered she had mysteriously contracted what is colloquially known as "the crabs." Being unsure of what course of action she should take, she went to the local Wal-Mart and told the first employee she encountered, "I have bugs in my bush."

The ever-helpful employee directed the woman to the Garden Center, where she told the supervisor, "I have bugs in my bush."

The Garden Center supervisor picked up a bottle of pesticide and told the woman, "This stuff will take care of any bugs you've got in your bush, your lawn, your trees, anywhere."

The woman, elated, rushed home and applied her new "medicine."

A few days later, while visiting the Wal-Mart, the Garden Center supervisor asked if her bug problem had disappeared. She replied, "Bugs gone, bush gone, Jose's mustache gone."

A man was looking all over town to find a friend of his. He walked down the street and came to a barbershop.

He stuck his head inside and asked, "Bob Peters here?"

The barber replied, "Nah, we just do shaves and haircuts."

How do you make Holy Water?

Boil the hell out of it.

What's the difference between a woman and a computer?

A woman won't take a 3.5-inch floppy.

"It's just too hot to wear clothes today," said Jack as he stepped out of the shower. "Honey, what do you think the neighbors would think if I mowed the lawn like this?"

"Probably that I married you for your money."

Fr. McGillicudy couldn't get any money from his congregation, so he took a course in hypnotism.

At Sunday Mass McGillicudy waved his little watch from the pulpit, back and forth, back and forth.

He asked the members of the congregation to put five bucks in the basket and they all did.

He thought this was great.

The following Sunday he did the same thing only this time he asked for ten bucks and they all put ten bucks in the basket.

He thought this was really turning into something.

So the next Sunday he was swinging his watch back and forth, back and forth and he accidentally dropped it.

"Oh, shit," he said.

It cost him 2,000 bucks to clean up the church.

A man comes home from work and finds his wife admiring her breasts in the mirror. He asks, "What are you doing?"

She replies, "I went to the doctor today, and he told me I have the breasts of a 25 year old."

The husband retorts, "Well, what did he say about your 50 year old ass?"

She replied, "Frankly, dear, your name never came up."

It's the yearly party at the temple and they're having the drawing for the door prizes. Goldstein wins third prize and gets a color TV. Rosenberg wins second prize, goes up to collect, and it's a plate of cookies.

He comes back to the table and says, "Goldstein, I don't understand it. You won third prize, you got a color TV. I won second prize, I got a god-damned plate of cookies."

Goldstein says, "Rosenberg, you don't understand. The plate of cookies was cooked by the Rabbi's wife."

Rosenberg says, "Fuck the Rabbi's wife!"

Goldstein whispers, "Shhh -- that's first prize!"

"How come you always give AOL members the bad jokes? That's discrimination."

Humr Grl with AOL
how come you always give AOL members the bad jokes? That's discrimination.

You're right. It is discrimination. But, fortunately, it's a LEGAL form of discrimination. Let me tell you why:

In the United States, it is illegal to discriminate on the basis of race, gender, sexual orientation, or religious background/beliefs. (My pre-Joke A Day life was in Human Resources.)

But it's not illegal to discriminate against people who have single digit (or negative integer) IQs. If you look at this url: http://www.aol.com/membershiprolls.htm you'll find all of the members of AOL categorized in many different ways -- INCLUDING IQ scores. (If you can't find that URL, look under http://www.aol.com/asuckereveryminute.htm)

Now, while there are undoubtedly many, many people on AOL who do have more intelligence than a hubcap (I myself have an AOL account and have had one for years to check the formatting of the information I send to AOL members), the vast majority of AOLiens are five beers short of a six-pack.

So, that's why AOLiens are discriminated against. It's legal. It's fun. It's easy. There's no end to the number of AOLiens because S. Case and company sign 'em up at a frantic pace. It gives the rest of the intelligent world a cyber-freak show to watch and laugh at.

. . . wait a minute . . . my trusty assistant just handed me a note . . . really? . . . you're kidding . . . huh . . . she just told me we send the SAME jokes to the AOL list as we do everyone else . . . OHHHH -- I see! OK! I'll pass this along to Humr:

*She told me that it's the SAME jokes, but that you've got to put the special AOL filter on your email program! Yeah, it's a special filter that actually lowers the comprehension level of the joke down to 2nd grader level -- thus allowing the masses at AOL to read and enjoy the humor without all of those annoying "big words" and "conceptual humor" that makes you **think** you're getting the "bad" jokes.*

*AOL, naturally, doesn't sell the filter directly, so if you want, send me the $39.95, and I'll get that filter off to you **today** and you, too, can be enjoying humor that **you** will be able to understand!*

Regards,

Ray
Joke A Day

Kelly with WebTv
dont get me wrong, ive been a big fan of joke a day since ive recieved it. problem is, todays joke, the first one. well ive heard it b4, and the version i heard it was much better. u have so many additives in this one. like, so many things were added since the original version and though if tactful enough additives can make a joke even funnier, u really ruined this one. the simplistic version was really a classic :-(

*Then, Kel, start your **own** list and tell 'em better.*

:)

look mr attitude it was constructive criticism and unless your mr jerry sienfeld yourself the lesson to be learned is : dont try and better the jokes, theyre funny as they were in their original state!!!!!!!!!!!! but thanx for the attitude anyway.....ray

Look, Ms. Humor impaired:

*(1) You didn't send **your** version so one could make a judgment about which one was funnier.*

(2) Humor is subjective and it's in the eyes of reader as to what's funny or not.

(3) Follow my ORIGINAL suggestion if you think you can do a better job. No attitude to that -- just a challenge. If you think your jokes are that much funnier, then YOU go do it better.

and another thing to your "chanlenge" is im not trying to compete with u. yeah start my own list, please, i smoke up so much weed i cant remember a joke i heard yesterday but in this case, my grandfather has been telling that joke everytime icome visit him for the past freakin 18 years so ill mention your 'challenge' to him but i doubt his the least bit concerned

"Forrest Gump dies and goes to heaven . . ."

Forrest Gump dies and goes to heaven. St. Peter greets him and says, "Heaven is so full that we have to give you an entrance exam to come in."

Forrest replies, "I shore hope it isn't too hard I'm not very good at tests."

St. Peter says: "First question, how many days in the week begin with T and what are they?"

Forrest answers: "Well, two, today and tomorrow."

"That isn't quite what I had in mind but, I'll give it to you," St. Peter said. "OK, the next question: how many seconds are there in a year?"

Forrest thought for a minute and said, "Well, I reckon there are twelve. January 2nd, February 2nd, March 2nd . . ."

St. Peter put up his hand. "Well, not the answer I was looking for, but it is correct so I'll have to give that one to you also. OK, final question: What is God's first name?"

"Well, that's easy. It's Howard."

"Howard? How in Heaven did you come up with Howard?"

"You know, 'Our Father, Who art in Heaven, Howard be Thy name.'"

Two boll weevils grew up in South Carolina. One went to Hollywood and became a famous actor. The other stayed behind in the cotton fields and never amounted to much.

The second one, naturally, became known as the lesser of two weevils.

Have you heard of the untimely passing of the Energizer Bunny?

Someone put his batteries in backwards and he just kept coming, and coming, and coming . . .

Former Vice President Quayle, former Speaker of the House Gingrich, and President Clinton are traveling in a car together in Kansas.

A tornado comes along and whirls them up into the air and tosses them thousands of yards away. They all fall into a daze.

When they come to, they extract themselves from the vehicle, and realize they're in the fabled Land of Oz.

They decide to go see the famous Wizard of Oz. The Wizard is known for granting people their wishes.

Quayle says, "I'm going to ask the Wizard for a brain."

Gingrich responds, "I'm going to ask the Wizard for a heart."

Clinton speaks up, "Where's Dorothy?"

I'm frequently asked, "Where do you find all of your jokes?" The answer: tons of places. Naturally, there are other humor lists that I'm a member of (though they rarely come through with something I've not seen -- and most of the time the stuff that appears in Joke A Day appears in theirs, just days later), there's magazines galore (is there any magazine that couldn't be helped with a "joke section"? C'mon, Time *and* People, *get on the ball here!) and books. I was in the library some time ago and picked up a book of jokes from the 19th century. I leafed through it and was amazed to find that many of the jokes I'm repeating today were in that book -- just with different names. That's the same with this joke above. It wasn't about the Wizard of Oz, naturally, but it used the very same kind of setup. It's my opinion that there really are no new jokes. Just new audiences.*

An Indian and a priest are walking through the woods. The priest is teaching the Indian the English language, so he can be integrated into the "white man's society."

As they walk along, the priest sees a tree and says to the Indian, "Tree." They continue walking along and come upon a bush, and the priest says to the Indian, "Bush." They keep walking and eventually come out into a small clearing, where they come upon a man and a woman having sex. The priest is so upset, he's not sure what he should tell the Indian. The only thing he can think of to say is "man riding a bicycle."

The Indian then pulls out his bow and arrow, aims and instantly kills the man. The priest turns to the Indian and says, "What'd you do that for?"

The Indian replies, "MY bicycle!!"

A man walked into a Doctor's office. "What do you have?" the receptionist asked.

"Shingles," he replied.

She told him to sit down. Soon a nurse called him and asked, "What do you have?"

"Shingles," he replied.

She took his blood pressure, weight, and complete medical history. Then she took him to a room and told him to remove all of his clothes. After a few minutes the Doctor came in and asked, "What do you have?"

"Shingles," the man told him.

The Doctor looked him up and down and said, "Where?"

"Out on the truck. Where do you want me to unload them?"

A doctor had the reputation of helping couples increase the joy in their sex life, but always promised not to take a case if he felt he could not help them. The Browns came to see the doctor, and he gave them thorough physical exams, psychological exams, and various tests and then concluded, "Yes, I am happy to say that I believe I can help you. On your way home from my office stop at the grocery store and buy some grapes and some doughnuts. Go home, take off your clothes, and you, sir, roll the grapes across the floor until you make a bull's eye in your wife's love canal. Then on hands and knees you must crawl to her like a leopard and retrieve the grape using only your tongue."

"Then next, ma'am, you must take the doughnuts and from across the room, toss them at your husband until you make a ringer around his love pole. Then like a lioness, you must crawl to him and consume the doughnut." The couple went home and their sex life became more and more wonderful.

They told their friends, Mr. & Mrs. Green, that they should see the good doctor. The doctor greeted the Greens and said he would not take the case unless he felt that he could help them; so he conducted the physical exams and the same battery of tests.

Then he told the Greens the bad news. "I cannot help you, so I will not take your money. I believe your sex life is as good as it will ever be. I cannot help."

The Greens pleaded with him, and said, "You helped our friends the Browns; now please, please help us."

"Well, all right," the doctor said. "On your way home from the office, stop at the grocery store and buy some apples and a box of Cheerios..."

This woman is sitting in a bar, wearing a tube top. She has never shaved her armpits in her entire life, so as a result, she has a thick black bush under each arm. Every 20 minutes, she raises her arm up and flags the bartender for another drink.

This goes on all night. The other people in the bar see her hairy pits every time she raises her arm. Near the end of the night, a drunk at the end of the bar says to the bartender, "Hey, I'd like to buy the ballerina a drink." The bartender replies, "What makes you think she's a ballerina?" The drunk says, "Any girl that can lift her leg that high has to be a ballerina!"

The grizzled old sea captain was quizzing a young naval student. "What steps would you take if a sudden storm came up on the starboard?"

"I'd throw out an anchor, sir."

"What would you do if another storm sprang up aft?"

"I'd throw out another anchor, sir."

"But what if a third storm sprang up forward?"

"I'd throw out another anchor, captain."

"Just a minute, son. Where in the world are you getting all these anchors?"

"From the same place you're getting all your storms, sir."

A retirement village decided to hold a Singles Dance, at which this very sweet 90-year-old gentleman met a very sweet 90-year-old lady, and they danced and talked and laughed, and just hit it off great.

They continued to see each other for a while and enjoyed each other so much, and danced so well together, etc., that they decided to get married.

On their wedding night, they went to bed and he reached over and took her hand and squeezed it, and she squeezed his hand back, and they went to sleep.

On the second night, when they went to bed, he reached over and squeezed her hand, and she squeezed his hand back, and they went to sleep.

On the third night, he reached over and took her hand, and she said, "Not tonight, Honey, I have a headache."

A boy is watching television and hears the name Jesus Christ. Wondering who Jesus Christ is, he asks his mother. She tells him that she is busy, and to ask his father. His father is also busy so he asks his brother. His brother kicks him out of the room because he doesn't have time to answer his stupid questions, so he goes downtown and sees a bum in an alley.

He asks the bum, "Who's Jesus Christ?" and the bum replies, "Well, I am."

The boy, not believing the bum, asks for proof. So the bum takes the boy into the bar down the street and takes him inside. They walk up to the bar and the bartender exclaims, "Jesus Christ, are you in here again?"

Visiting a lawyer for advice, the wife said, "I want you to help me obtain a divorce. My husband is getting a little queer to sleep with."

"What do you mean?" asked the attorney. "Does he force you to indulge in unusual sex practices?"

"No, he doesn't," replied the woman, "and neither does the little queer."

A White man and a Black man race on foot through a tunnel.
Who wins?

The White man; the Black man stopped to write "motherfucker" on the wall.

As I was compiling jokes for this book, I was slightly amazed that I'd at one time told this one. A couple of months later I told another one similar to it:

Once God decided all people should look the same so there's no difference and discrimination among them. He also was quite pissed at them and so he turned all humans into cows.

The cows were all of the same color and you couldn't tell one from another.

So one day a cow walks to another and says, "Mooooo."

The other replies, "Moooo, motherfucker!"

There's no way on earth I could get away with these jokes today. The audience is just too damned big and there are too many "politically correct" idiots in the world for it to work. Curiously, many of my African American (OK, hell, let's say "Black") readers frequently write me and ask for jokes just like this. Funny how it's always the "politically correct" folks who are offended.

Two men are sitting in a pub talking. One mentions that it's his wife's birthday soon and he doesn't know what to get her.

The second man says that he bought his wife a blue Porsche and a red Porsche for her birthday because if she didn't like the blue one, she could have the red one, and vice versa.

The next week, the second man asks the other what he finally bought his wife.

He replies, "A necklace and a vibrator."

"Why?" asks the second man.

To which the other man replies, "Because if she doesn't like the necklace, she can go fuck herself."

As the pastor shook hands with the congregation leaving the church, a little boy looked up with a closed fist said, "Here, I have something for you." The pastor opened his hand and the little boy dropped a quarter in the pastor's hand. Not wanting to hurt the boy's feelings he simply smiled and said, "Thank you."

Well, it did not end. The next Sunday and the next -- the same thing. Finally, the pastor could not take it any more; he had to know what was up. He called the boy aside and talked with him, "I really appreciate the gifts but why are you doing it?"

"Well," said the boy, "I just wanted to help you -- my dad says you are the poorest preacher we have ever had."

While sports fishing off the Florida coast, a tourist capsized his boat. He could swim, but his fear of alligators kept him clinging to the overturned craft. Spotting an old beachcomber standing on the shore, the tourist shouted, "Are there any 'gators around here?!"

"Naw," the man hollered back, "they ain't been around for years!"

Feeling safe, the tourist started swimming leisurely toward the shore.

About halfway there he asked the guy, "How'd you get rid of the 'gators?"

"We didn't do nothin'," the beachcomber said. "The sharks got 'em."

Two cows are chewing their cuds, when one leans over to the other and asks her what she thinks about mad cow disease.

The other leans back and replies: "Cows, what do I care about cows? I'm a helicopter."

With the sun beginning to rise, the cabin of the jetliner was suddenly illuminated. "Who turned on the fucking lights?" a male passenger, who had been surly since boarding, snarled at a stewardess.

The girl had had enough of this particular character. "These are the breakfast lights, sir," she answered with forced sweetness. "The fucking lights are much dimmer, and you snored right through them."

George was using the gents in San Diego. Next to him was a large black man. George kept sneaking a peek at the man's penis.

The black man got angry and asked George what in the hell he thought he was looking at.

George said "Excuse me but I was looking at your . . . thing. How come all you black men have such big ones?"

The black man replied, "It's easy really, just go home and hang a three pound weight from it."

A couple of weeks later, George was walking down the street, and saw the same black man. "Hi Bro, how's your thing?" asked the black man.

Old George said, "I'm half way there."

"How's that, bro?" asked the black man.

George replied, "Well, it's turned black."

There was this boss screwing his secretary. She came into work every day one week at 10:30 instead of 8:00 like she was supposed to. He asked her, "Who said you could come in any time you wanted?"

She replied, "My lawyer."

Three men of the cloth -- a Catholic priest, a Baptist minister and a Rabbi -- were counting collections taken during services for the week. They were trying to come up with an equitable way to divide the money between God (the two churches and one synagogue) and themselves (the clerics' weekly income).

The priest was the first to speak: "I know what! I'll draw a line down the middle of the sanctuary, toss the money up in the air, and whatever falls on the right side of the line is for God and whatever falls on the left side is for us."

The Baptist minister cried, "No! No! No! I'll draw a circle in the middle of the sanctuary, toss the money up in the air, and whatever falls inside the circle is for God and whatever falls outside the circle is for us."

The Rabbi then asked the two other men to accompany him outside. There he offered this suggestion: "What I would do with the money is this: Toss it up in the air, and whatever God catches is His and whatever falls on the ground is ours."

Everyone farts, admit it or not. Kings fart, queens fart. Edward Lear, the 19th century English landscape painter, wrote affectionately of a favorite Duchess who gave enormous dinner parties attended by the cream of society.

One night she let out a ripper and quick as a flash she turned her gaze to her stoic butler, standing, as always, behind her.

"Hawkins!" she cried, "Stop that!"

"Certainly, your Grace," he replied with unhurried dignity, "Which way did it go?"

Man, I've been a long-winded sucker in this chapter, haven't I?

Back to "Where do I get my jokes" -- this one came from a book called The Complete Fart Book. *Man, they'll publish anything, huh? You're holding proof of that . . .*

Jon had always wanted to be an actor, but never succeeded because he had a hard time remembering lines. A friend of his, Judi, told him about a bit part in a community play. She assured Jon that he could do it because he'd only have to remember one line.

Jon decided to take the part. His only line was, "Hark, I hear the cannons roar!"

Jon practiced and practiced, "Hark, I hear the cannons roar!"

The opening night of the play Jon was very nervous.

Backstage, he practiced his line, over and over again, "Hark, I hear the cannons roar! Hark, I hear the cannons roar!"

Jon was given his cue and went on stage. He hears a loud BOOM, and yells, "WHAT THE HELL WAS THAT?"

The ambitious coach of a girls' track team gives the squad steroids. The team's performance soars. They win the county and state championship until one day they are favored to win nationals easily.

Penelope, a sixteen-year-old hurdler, visits her coach and says, "Coach, I have a problem. Hair is starting to grow on my chest."

"What!" the coach says in a panic, "How far down does it go?"

She replies, "Down to my balls. That's something else I want to talk to you about."

Mrs. O'Donovan was walking down O'Connell Street in Dublin, and coming in the opposite direction was Father O'Rafferty.

"Hello," said the Father, "And how is Mrs. O'Donovan? Didn't I marry you two years ago?"

"You did that, Father."

"And are there any little ones yet?"

"No, not yet, Father," said she.

"Well, now, I'm going to Rome next week, and I'll light a candle for you."

"Thank you, Father." And away she went.

A few years later they met again.

"Well now, Mrs. O'Donovan," said the Father, "how are you?"

"Oh, very well," said she.

"And tell me," he said, "have you any little ones yet?"

"Oh yes, Father. I've had three sets of twins, and four singles -- ten in all."

"Now isn't that wonderful," he said "And how is your lovely husband?"

"Oh," she said, "he's over in Rome to blow that bloody candle out!"

An old couple head to the doctor for their annual physicals. One at a time, the doctor brings them into the examination room, starting with the husband.

"Well, Mr. Smith, you're in great shape for a man your age," says the doctor.

The man replies, "Well doc, I don't drink, I don't smoke, and the good Lord looks out for me."

"What do you mean?" asks the doctor.

The old man says, "For instance, last night in the middle of the night, I had to get up to go to the bathroom and the good Lord turned on the light for me so I wouldn't fall down."

"That's nice," said the doctor, confused. "Send your wife in now, please."

The wife comes in and the doc says, "Mrs. Smith, you're in great shape for a woman your age."

She then says, "Well, doc, I don't drink, I don't smoke . . ."

The doctor interrupts, "And the good Lord looks after you, right?"

The woman is confused and says, "What are you talking about?"

The doctor explains, "Your husband was just telling me the same thing. He said that the good Lord looks after him. Like last night when he had to go to the bathroom, the good Lord turned the light on for him."

"Damn!" she yelled, "So he's pissing in the refrigerator again!"

A salesman rang the bell at a suburban home, and was greeted by a nine-year-old boy puffing on a long black cigar.

Hiding his amazement, the salesman asked the boy, "Is your mother home?"

The boy took the cigar out of his mouth, flicked ashes on the carpet, and asked, "What do *you* think?"

The first mate was found drunk on duty one day. The Captain ordered the offense to be written into the log. So, into the official ship's log was written, "The first mate was drunk today."

The first mate begged and pleaded to the captain to remove that entry but the captain argued that once an entry was made in the log it couldn't be deleted. The first mate decided to get even.

The next day the first mate had the duty of keeping the log. In it he wrote, "The Captain was sober today."

"*Too bad for you ya shitbags!*"

cheerkmw with hotmail
i got an idea. how about you shut the fuck up all you pieces of shit. i am going to send a fucking virus to you now! so haha. too bad for you ya shitbags!!!!!!!!

Always good to hear from you, Mom . . .

Karen with kenton
Hello, Ray! I sent you a message at the "help" address, but I guess that was a bad idea. Here's the gist:

I've always enjoyed Joke-a-Day, but I didn't care for the political twist of today's installment. Really, I don't share your conservative politics, and I don't subscribe to this service to be exposed to the Jesse Helms/Strom Thurmond/Trent Lott/Newt Gingrich type of viewpoint. I hate those guys -- but I like you!

On the plus side, I have really appreciated Joke-A-Day, which often perks me up and gives me a joke to share with coworkers and classmates. (I'm a graduate student in poetry, which is a joke in and of itself!) So keep it coming -- unless it's more political silliness. Any more in this vein and I'll have to unsubscribe.

In closing, I hope you don't find my comments too abrasive. I just wanted to provide you with some possibly helpful feedback, since I was a bit disgruntled at today's installment.

Karen:

You've stated something that similar folks have today (about 5 others) except you accomplished it a little more politely than they did. So that's why I won't just automatically tell ya to "pound sand" as I did those other folks. .

*But the bottom line is this: I'll print my grocery list if I want to. As the publisher, editor, and owner of Joke A Day, I'll print anything I see fit. My **only** guideline that I follow to the letter is: it must make me laugh. The article today did just that. It also coincidentally went right down the line with my views on those subjects.*

What I simply don't understand is how anyone can disagree with them. Oh, the other writers brought up the argument, "Well, what happens to the sick, the infirm, the ones who can't work?" I say: We take care of them. That's what government is FOR. Taking care of the people who cannot take care of themselves. Catch the keyword in that sentence, though: "cannot."

My mother, for instance, is 63 years old and she cannot work. (She can't stand for more than about 5 minutes at a stretch and has a number of health problems. These make her one step away from being bed-ridden.) I'm all for the government giving her a helping hand. (She's eligible for and does draw Social Security.)

But I would NOT expect the government to be her sole source of support. I send her money every month, my brother helps out with paying for different items, and my sisters (who still live in our hometown) visit and take care of still other things. (My father passed away several years ago.)

Ahhh, but what about those who truly HAVE no one else? If they truly have no one else AND they cannot take care of themselves, then "the people" should band together and take care of them.

But, I'm not talking about providing a mansion. I mean we should take care of the basics. A decent place to live. Food so they won't be hungry. Medical care so a person isn't sick. That's what "government" should be about.

I'm all for locking people away who commit crimes. I'm all for executing someone who kills or rapes someone I love. I'm all for people taking responsibility for THEMSELVES and their family and NOT rely on the government as the provider of first choice.

How could you possibly disagree with my sentiments?

Finally, if you don't agree with my right as the owner of this publication to print whatever I want to print, then I will issue you an invitation to unsubscribe now. I tell jokes here on a more than routine basis. That's what keeps the customers coming back and that's what pays the bills around here. It would be insane to change the formula. I don't even WANT to change the formula. I love telling jokes.

But, what sets me apart from every other humor mailing list on the planet is this: what you see here is real. What I tell people is real. I put out my personality day in and day out on this list. I "talk" to the readers as if I was sitting across from them. There's absolutely no other way for me to do this except being as personal and personable as I can. It's the reason why Joke A Day went from being a nothing little 3rd rate humor list to the largest one in the world in an incredibly short amount of time -- I'm not afraid to tell people what I think, how I feel, or what my views are on certain subjects.

You won't find that anywhere else.

Take care. Check your "political correctness" at the door the next time I go off in a different direction than yours. You state you like the humor (and you like me personally -- that's pretty cool) so unsubscribing would simply hurt yourself. I'm going to keep on keeping on just the way I've always done it.

Ray
Joke A Day

Karen in New Zealand
Dear Ray - just a note to thank you for your site and especially the letters. I really look forward to Thursday when I can read the updated ones. Today more so for the following reasons: Our new business is going well but some income would be appreciated - its been 3 months now and of course, things are starting to get tight. Then this morning, my washing machine decided that it was sick of draining the water out and going into the spin cycle with a full tank would be the go. Have you ever seen what happens to water when its spun at high speed? Yup

- up and out. The laundry is super clean, my washing still wet. Then my precious 7 year old came out with a photo taken of me when I was 21 (I'm only 34 now) and said "Look a picture of you in the Olden Days"! My son fell off the fence, and his twin won't go to bed. Sigh - you see why I need a fix of escapism. Well - now I'm off for a fag and a cup of whatever alcohol I can find - with my luck it will be damn cooking sherry.

"There was a little old lady on the corner . . ."

There was a little old lady on the corner; she had both hands holding her hat on while the wind blew her skirt up around her face.

A dignified southern gentleman came up and said, "Ma'am, you should be ashamed of yourself, letting your skirt blow around, being indecent, while both hands hold your hat."

She said, "Look, everything down there is eighty years old; this hat is brand new!"

Jon: "I'm calling because I read your ad for someone to retail canaries."

Store owner: "And you want the job?"

Jon: "No, I'd just like to know how the canaries lost their tails."

Blonde to another Blonde, "Could you lend me $40 and only give me half now. This way I will owe you $20 and you will owe me $20 and we will be even."

Young Dave was courting Mabel, who lived on an adjoining farm out west in cattle country. One evening, as they were sitting on Dave's porch watching the sun go down over the hills, Dave spied his prize bull doing the business on one of his cows.

He sighed in contentment at this idyllic rural scene and figured the omens were right for him to put the hard word on Mabel.

He leaned in close and whispered in her ear, "Mabel, I'd sure like to be doing what that bull is doing."

"Well then, why don't you? "Mabel whispered back. "It is YOUR cow."

A man was bragging about his sister who had disguised herself as a man and joined the army.

"But, wait a minute," said the listener, "She'll have to dress with the boys and shower with them too. Won't she?"

"Sure," replied the man.

"Well, won't they find out?"

The man shrugged. "But who'll tell?"

On preparing to return home from an out-of-town trip, this man got a small puppy as a present for his son. Not having time to get the paper work to take the puppy onboard, the man just hid the pup down the front of his pants and snuck him onboard the airplane.

About 30 minutes into the trip a flight attendant noticed the man shaking and quivering.

"Are you OK, Sir?" asked the attendant.

"Yes, I'm fine," said the man.

Sometime later the attendant noticed the man moaning, and shaking again. "Are you sure you're all right, Sir?"

"Yes," said the man, "but I have a confession to make. I didn't have time to get the paperwork to bring a puppy onboard, so I hid him down the front of my pants."

"What's wrong?" asked the stew, "Is he not house-broken?"

"No, that's not the problem. The problem is he's not weaned yet!"

A farmer had so many children he ran out of names, so he started naming his kids after something around the farm. The first day of school began, and the teacher asked each child his name. When he got to one of the farmer's sons, the boy replied, "Wagon Wheel."

The teacher said, "I need your REAL name, son," to which the boy replied, "It's Wagon Wheel, Sir...Really."

The teacher, in a huff, said, "All right young man! March yourself right down to the principal's office THIS minute!!!!"

The boy got out of his chair...turned to his sister and said, "Come on, Chicken Shit; he ain't gonna believe YOU, neither!"

Haircuts -- The difference between men and women

Women's version:
==================
Woman2: Oh! You got a haircut! That's so cute!

Woman1: Do you think so? I wasn't sure when she gave me the mirror. I mean, you don't think it's too fluffy looking?

Woman2: Oh God no! No, it's perfect. I'd love to get my hair cut like that, but I think my face is too wide. I'm pretty much stuck with this stuff I think.

Woman1: Are you serious? I think your face is adorable. And you could easily get one of those layer cuts -- that would look so cute I think. I was actually going to do that except that I was afraid it would accent my long neck.

Woman2: Oh -- that's funny! I would love to have your neck! Anything to take attention away from this two-by-four I have for a shoulder line.

Woman1: Are you kidding? I know girls that would love to have your shoulders. Everything drapes so well on you. I mean, look at my arms -- see how short they are? If I had your shoulders I could get clothes to fit me so much easier...

- - - - - - - - - - - - - - - -

Men's version:

===============

Man2: Haircut?
Man1: Yeah.

After I read this one to my "then wife" she gave me one of "those looks" that told me this joke hit a little too close to home to be all that funny to her. Probably why she's my "then wife" and not my "now wife," huh?

Anyway, a couple of weeks after I told it, we were in Red Lobster. There were two tables of ladies adjacent to ours. One group got up and realized they knew the other group. Lots of "oh, wow, we didn't see you sitting here" bullshit.

One lady noticed the hairstyle of another and, I swear, launched into an almost word for word rendition of the joke above. I just howled my ass off and gave my "then wife" one of "those looks."

A herd of buffalo can only move as fast as the slowest buffalo, much like the brain can only operate as fast as the slowest brain cells. The slowest buffalo are the sick and weak so they die off first, making it possible for the herd to move at a faster pace.

Like the buffalo, the weak, slow brain cells are the ones that are killed off by excessive beer drinking and socializing, making the brain operate faster.

The moral of the story: Drink more beer, it will make you smarter.

A woman was sick of her husband's drinking, so she decided to teach him a lesson. She dressed up like Satan, and when her husband returned home from another bender, she jumped out from behind the sofa and screamed.

"You don't scare me," the man said, looking her over calmly. "I married your sister."

Did you hear about the new all-female delivery service?
It's called UPMS -- they deliver whenever the hell they feel like it.

Two bees buzz around what's left of a rose bush. "How was your summer?" Bee #1 asks.

"Not too good," says Bee #2. "Lotta rain, lotta cold. Not enough flowers, not enough pollen."

The first bee has an idea. "Hey, why don't you go down the corner and hang a left? There's a bar mitzvah going on. Plenty of flowers and fruit."

Bee #2 buzzes, "Thanks!" and takes off.

An hour later, the bees bump into each other again. "How was the bar mitzvah?" asks Bee #1.

"Great!" says Bee #2.
The first bee peers at his pal and wonders, "What's that on your head?"

"A yarmulke," is the answer. "I didn't want them to think I was a wasp."

Jon takes his dog for a walk. After awhile he gets thirsty so he ties his dog to a parking meter in front of a bar and goes in for a couple of beers. After he has been there for an hour or so the local policeman enters the bar.

"Whose dog is tied up out front?"

Jon responds, "That's my dog. Is there a problem, officer?"

"Well, she's in heat," says the cop.

"Oh, she'll be all right. It's shady out there."

"That's not what I mean. Your dog needs bred."

"I gave her a half of a loaf this morning. She's fine."

At this point the policeman is becoming a little upset. "Listen, fellow. You don't seem to understand what I am talking about. That dog needs to be screwed."

"Go right ahead, officer, I've always wanted a police dog."

There was this Christian lady that had to do a lot of traveling for her business so she did a lot of flying. But flying made her nervous so she always took her Bible along with her to read and it helped relax her. One time she was sitting next to a man. When he saw her pull out her Bible he gave a little chuckle and went back to what he was doing.

After a while he turned to her and asked, "You don't really believe all that stuff in there do you?"

The lady replied, "Of course I do. It is the Bible."
He said, "Well, what about that guy that was swallowed by that whale?"

She replied, "Oh, Jonah. Yes I believe that, it is in the Bible."

He asked, "Well, how do you suppose he survived all that time inside the whale?"

The lady said, "Well, I don't really know.   I guess when I get to Heaven I will ask him."

"What if he isn't in Heaven?" the man asked sarcastically.

"Then you can ask him," replied the lady.

A man decides to take the opportunity while his wife is away to paint the toilet seat.   The wife comes home sooner than expected, sits, and gets the seat stuck to her rear.   She is understandably distraught about this and asks her husband to drive her to the doctor.

She puts on a large overcoat so as to cover the stuck seat, and they go. When they get to the doctor's, the man lifts his wife's coat to show their predicament. The man asks, "Doctor, have you ever seen anything like this before?"

"Well, yes," the doctor replies, "but never framed."

A psychiatrist's secretary walks into his study and says, "There's a gentleman in the waiting room asking to see you.   Claims he's invisible."

The psychiatrist responds, "Tell him I can't see him."

A guy is walking down the street and enters a clock and watch shop. While looking around, he notices a drop dead gorgeous female clerk behind the counter.

He walks up to the counter where she is standing, unzips his pants, and places his dick on the counter.

"What are you doing, Sir?" she asks. "This is a clock shop!!"

He replied, "I know it is. And I would like 2 hands and a face put on THIS!!"

Two cab drivers met. "Hey," asked one, "what's the idea of painting one side of your cab red and the other side blue?"

"Well," the other responded, "when I get into an accident, you should see how all the witnesses contradict each other."

Having flashed his light into the back of a parked mini-van behind a local burger joint, the policeman gasped, "Are you two actually having sex in the parking lot?"

"Why no, officer." drawled the sweet young thing. "This here fellow is just helping me practice in case I meet a strong handsome policeman I could really go for."

A priest went into the country to pay a visit to a 92-year-old church member whom he had not seen for some years. She welcomed him into the parlor. While she made tea, he looked around and saw a beautiful oak pump organ with a cut glass bowl sitting on top of it. The bowl was half-filled with water and a condom was floating on top of it. Astonished and shocked, he quickly turned away. But after tea, curiosity got the best of him, and he asked her about it.

"Oh, yes," she said enthusiastically. "While in town last year I found a package on the sidewalk. The directions on the back said, 'Keep wet and put on your organ to prevent disease.' And you know, I think it works. I haven't had a cold all winter!"

Two sailors on shore leave are walking down the street. They spot a beautiful blonde, and the first sailor asks his friend, "Have you ever slept with a blonde?"

The second sailor replies that he has.

First: "Have you ever slept with a brunette?"

Second: "Why yes, in fact, I've slept with brunettes on several occasions."

They walk on a little farther and see a gorgeous redhead who makes the other two women look dowdy.

First: "Have you ever slept with a redhead then?"

His companion looks at him and answers slowly, "Not a wink!"

*One of the best things I ever heard about brunettes was this: "There's no one better to have next to your bed if you're sick and no one better to have **in** your bed if you're not."*

*I had a very sexy redheaded friend who told me once, "With a blonde or a brunette, you get out of bed when you're satisfied.   With a redhead, you get out of bed when **she's** satisfied."*

Two young men, who had just graduated from Harvard, were all excited and talking effusively as they got into a taxi in downtown Boston. After hearing them for a couple of minutes the cab driver asked, "You men Harvard graduates?"
"Yes, Sir! Class of '98!" they answered proudly.

The cab driver extended his hand back to shake their hands, saying, "Class of '58."

A Briton, a Frenchman and a Russian are viewing a painting of Adam and Eve frolicking in the Garden of Eden.

"Look at their reserve, their calm," muses the Brit. "They must be British."

"Nonsense," the Frenchman disagrees.   "They're naked, and so beautiful. Clearly, they are French."

"No clothes, no shelter," the Russian points out, "they have only an apple to eat, and they're being told this is Paradise. They are Russian."

A traveling salesman was about to check in at a hotel when he noticed a very charming bit of femininity giving him the so-called "glad eye."

In a casual manner he walked over and spoke to her as though he had known her all his life. Both walked back to the desk and registered as Mr. and Mrs.

After a three-day stay he walked up to the desk and informed the clerk that he was checking out. The clerk presented him with his bill for $1600.

"There is a mistake here," he protested. "I have been here only three days."

"Yes," replied the clerk, "but your wife has been here a month."

An 8 year old girl goes to her dad who is working in the yard and asks, "Daddy, what's sex?"

The father is surprised that she would ask such a question, but decides that if she is old enough to ask the question, then she is old enough to get a straight answer.

He tells her about the birds and the bees; the egg and the sperm; and the male and female. When he has finished explaining, the little girl is looking at him with her mouth opened, so the father asks her, "Why did you ask this question?"

The little girl explains that "Mom told me to tell you that dinner would be ready in just a couple of secs."

Fellow 1: "Boy my wife makes me mad! I really feel like telling her off again."

Fellow 2: "What do you mean again?"

Fellow 1: "I felt like telling her off yesterday, too."

Two gay men were visiting a zoo, when they found themselves at the gorilla cage. The gorilla was sitting there with a huge erection. Unable to contain himself, one of the men reaches in to touch it.

As soon as his arm goes into the cage, the gorilla grabs him, and takes him into the cage, slams him to the floor and fucks him senseless.

A few days later in hospital the boyfriend visits and asks his partner if he is hurt.

"Hurt? Hurt? You bet I'm hurt. He hasn't phoned, he hasn't written . . ."

A lion in the London zoo was lying in the sun licking its arse when a visitor turned to the keeper and said, "That's a docile old thing isn't it?"

"No way," said the keeper, "it's the most ferocious beast in the zoo. Why, just an hour ago it dragged an Australian tourist into the cage and completely devoured him."

"Hardly seems possible," said the astonished visitor, "but why is it lying there licking its arse?"

"The poor thing is trying to get the taste out of its mouth."

A tiny but dignified old lady was among a group looking at an art exhibition in a newly-opened gallery. Suddenly, one contemporary painting caught her eye.

"What on earth," she inquired of the artist standing nearby, "is that?"

He smiled condescendingly. "That, my dear lady, is supposed to be a mother and her child."

"Well, then," snapped the little old lady, "why isn't it?"

This fellow was walking home from work one evening, very depressed. He was married to a nagging woman who was constantly switching between treating him nice and tearing down his self-esteem. To add to it, his best friend was to be hanged that night for a capital crime.

He stomped into the house and slammed the door, sunk in his self-pity.

His wife said, "Honey, what's the problem?"

"They're hanging my best friend, Tony Wright, tonight!"

"I understand, go take a bath. I'll get supper ready for you, Sweetie, and you can go down to see him before the hanging. Now, won't that make you feel better?"

He decided to not make it worse and agreed with her proposal.

Well, while she was getting supper the paper came, hitting the front door with a plop. She picked it up and opened it. The heading said, "WRIGHT GETS STAY OF EXECUTION."

She knew her husband would want to know immediately and hearing the great news would really lift his spirits, so she went up the stairs and opened the bathroom door. There he was, bent over and naked, cleaning the tub.

She said, "Honey, they're not hanging Wright tonight!"

He answered, "The same old story. First you're nice and then bitch, bitch, bitch!!!"

A farmer rings up the vet and says "Two of me chickens have stopped laying."

The vet says, "Really, how do you know?"

The farmer says, "I just ran over the bastards in me tractor."

A foursome was on the last hole and when the last golfer drove off the tee he hooked into a cow pasture. He advised his friends to play through and he would meet them at the clubhouse. They followed the plan and waited for their friend. After a considerable time he appeared disheveled, bloody, and badly beaten up. They all wanted to know what happened.

He explained that he went over to the cow pasture but could not find his ball. He noticed a cow wringing her tail in obvious pain. He went over and lifted her tail and saw a golf ball solidly embedded.

It was a yellow Titleist so he knew it was not his. A woman came out of the bushes apparently searching for her lost golf ball.

The helpful male golfer lifted the cow's tail and asked, "Does this look like yours?" and that was the last thing he could remember.

There are two problems with attorney jokes:

1. Attorneys do not think they are funny, and

2. Most people do not understand that they are really jokes.

These two guys had just gotten divorced and they swore they would never have anything to do with women again. They were best friends and they decided to move up to Alaska, as far north as they could go, and never look at a woman again.

They got up there and went into a trader's store and told him, "Give us enough supplies to last two men for one year." The trader got the gear together and on top of each one's supplies he laid a board with a hole in it, with fur around the hole. The guys said, "What's that board for?"

The trader said, "Well, where you're going there are no women and you might need this."

They said, "No way! We've sworn off women for life!" The trader said, "Well, take the boards with you, and if you don't use them I'll refund your money next year."

"OK," they said and left.

Next year one of them came into the trader's store and said "Give me enough supplies to last one man for one year."

The trader said "Weren't you in here last year with a partner?"

"Yeah," said the guy.

"Where is he?" asked the trader.

"I shot him," said the guy.

"Why?"

"I caught him in bed with my board," was the reply.

Three men are traveling the Amazon; a German, an American, and a Polack. They get captured by some Amazons.

The head of the tribe asks the German, "What do you want on your back for your whipping?"

The German responds, "I will take oil!"

So they put oil on his back, and a large Amazon whips him 10 times. When he is finished the German has these huge welts on his back, and he can hardly move.

The Amazons haul the German away, and say to the Polack, "What do you want on your back?"

"I will take nothing!" says the Polack, and the Polack stands there straight and takes his 10 lashings without a single flinch.

"What will you take on your back?" the Amazons ask the American, who responds "I'll take the Polack!"

"OR I WILL TAKE MY BUSINESS ELSEWHERE."

Uklioness with AOL
PLEASE STOP SENDING ME THIS E-MAIL, OR I WILL TAKE MY BUSINESS ELSEWHERE. I HAVE MADE THIS REQUEST THREE TIMES ALREADY.

Wouldn't "taking your business elsewhere" be the same as unsubscribing?

Lori with gowebway
I get a special little tingle reading your letters every Wednesday! I work for that government agency now billed as "kinder and gentler." Sometimes I just want to grab some of these idiots by the collar, throw 'em face down in the dirt..and...oh, well, better not go there! But I have started thinking, while smiling secretly to myself, "Wonder how Ray would handle this wackadoo?"

Anyway, thanks, Ray, for making my day. Don't tell my boyfriend, but I do fantasize about a certain Jokemeister.....

Gerald made a mistake a lot of people do when they try to forward one of my mails -- they send me a copy of their reply. Someone forwarded him one of my jokes and he was writing back to that person:

Gerald with sky
LOL

I like the little girl joke!

I used to subscribe to jokeaday, but Ray was pissing me off with all his moaning and crying all the time, just because some people didn't appreciate some of his postings. I finally got to where I couldn't stand to read his crap anymore, and unsubscribed. I sure do miss those jokes though, so keep sending the good ones!

Any word on the girls?

love you!
Gerald

LOL!

Yeah, I like the part where the idiot forgets to check who he's sending mail to and misdirects a piece of mail back to ME. Boy, is HIS mailbox going to be stuffed when I post it on the Letters or Dweeb page this coming week and let the 200,000 or so folks on the list have a crack at HIM!

Any word on the lynchings?

Fondly,

Ray
Joke A Day

Ray!

ROFL

Well, I guess I deserve this one! See what happens when you work nights, and respond to email BEFORE your daily coffee? I guess I deserve what's coming to me, and I'll take it in good humor. Just remember this: I AM a postal worker, and I CAN get your addy!

Here's joking at you!

Gerald

Big deal. If you get here as fast as the mail does I'll have time to build a fortress. Brick by brick. With one hand tied behind my back. Blindfolded. Twice.

Besides, you misdirected the email to me. I have no faith the "snail mail" will arrive, either.

"This gay guy is in the doctor's office . . ."

This gay guy is in the doctor's office when the doc comes in and says, "I'm sorry, but you have contracted HIV."

The gay guy is immediately shocked and says, "Doc, Doc, what should I do?"

The doctor says, "Well, the first thing you should do is fly to Mexico. When you get there, eat all the Mexican food you can eat. Tacos, nachos, beans, and all that. Also, drink all the water you can, and none of that bottled crap, pure Mexican water, and as much as you can drink. Then eat all of the fresh fruit you can eat. Just keep eating and drinking the whole time you stay down there."

So the gay guy is a little confused, and asks, "So is all that going to help?"

The doc says, "No, but it will teach you what your asshole is used for."

A man walks into a pharmacy and wanders up and down the aisles.

The salesgirl notices him and asks if she can help him.

He answers that he is looking for a box of tampons for his wife. She directs him down the correct aisle. A few minutes later, he deposits a huge bag of cotton balls on the counter.

She says, confused, "Sir, I thought you were looking for tampons for your wife?"

"You see it's like this. Yesterday, I sent my wife to the store to get me a carton of cigarettes and she came home with a tin of tobacco and some rolling paper. So, I figure, if I have to roll my own, SO DOES SHE!"

Joe is having a drink in his local bar when in walks this gorgeous woman.

Joe, not being too shy, goes up and sits next to her.

He buys her a drink and then another and then another.

After this and the accompanying small talk, Joe asks her back to his place for a "good time."

"Look," says the woman, "what do you think I am? I don't turn into a slut after 3 drinks, you know!"

"OK," replies Joe, "so how many does it take?"

What does it mean when the Post Office flies the flag at half-mast?

"We're hiring!"

A couple was going to a costume party. The husband was unsure of what costume to wear. His wife was telling him to hurry or they would be late for the party. She was walking down the stairs from the bedroom, completely naked except on her feet were a big old floppy pair of boots.

"Where is your costume?" the husband asked.

"This is it," replied his wife.

"What the hell kind of costume is that???" asked the husband.

"Why, I am going as Puss and Boots," explained the wife. "Now hurry and get your costume on."

The husband went upstairs and was back in about 2 minutes. He also was completely naked except he had a rose vase slid over his penis.

"What the hell kind of costume is that???" asked the wife.

"I am a fire alarm," he replied.

"A fire alarm?" she repeated laughing.

"Yes," he replied. "In case of fire break the glass, pull twice and I come."

Guns don't kill people.
Husbands who come home early kill people.

The golf pro trying to teach the young miss the proper stance and swing had somehow gotten his zipper tangled in the back of her shorts. After many unsuccessful attempts to free it, the embarrassed couple lock-stepped to the clubhouse for assistance.

A German Shepherd laying on the lawn jumped up, got the garden hose, and turned it on them.

A major oil company discovered a large oil deposit on an Indian reservation. Their only problem was that they could not drill for the oil as long as one member of the tribe remained on the land. There was only one old Indian still living on the land and his name was Chief Bowels.

Chief Bowels was proving to be very stubborn about moving off of his tribal lands. The oil company offered him large sums of cash, stocks, and everything else they could think of but the only reply he ever gave them was, "Bowels no move!"

Then the lawyers discovered a clause in the treaty that allowed them to move the old chief off the land and into a rest home if he could no longer take care of himself.

The company sent Chief Bowels to a doctor hoping he could be shown to be an invalid. The doctor, not knowing what the situation was, asked the chief what the problem was.

The chief replied, "Bowels no move!"

The doctor gave the chief some laxative and sent him on his way. The next day the oil company sent Chief Bowels back to the doctor, hoping for better results. The doctor again asked the chief what the problem was.

The chief replied, "Bowels still no move!" So the doctor gave him some more laxatives and sent him on his way. This cycle continued for about two weeks.

Then one day the chief showed up as usual at the doctor's office. The doctor again asked what the problem was. The chief replied, "Bowels move. Bowels have to move. Teepee full of shit!"

Between her sophomore and junior years at college, my daughter Laurie waited tables at a rather seedy steak house. One evening she waited on a well-dressed young couple.

In a rather condescending tone, the man asked her, "Have you ever thought of going to college?"

"Actually, I DO go to college," Laurie replied.

"Well, I went to Harvard," he said, surveying the restaurant, "and I'd NEVER work in a place like this."

"I go to Vassar," Laurie retorted, "and I'd never EAT in a place like this."

It was the first day of school, and the elementary school teacher was establishing the fact that she'd take no nonsense from the kiddies this year. While taking the roll, she was told by one boy, "My name is Johnny Fuckhauer."

So she said, "There'll be none of that kind of thing this year, Johnny; tell me your REAL name!"

The kid said, "No, really teacher, it IS Johnny Fuckhauer. You can go across the hall to fourth grade and ask my brother if you don't believe me!"

Not wanting to be subjected to that kind of thing, the teacher went across the hall and knocked on the fourth grade classroom door. The fourth grade teacher had stepped down the hall to the front office for a moment, so she entered the room and directly asked the class, "Do you have a Fuckhauer in here?"

"Hell no!" replied a little kid from the front row, "We don't even get a cookie break!"

There was a middle-aged couple who had two stunningly beautiful blonde teenage daughters. They decided to try one last time for the son they always wanted.

After months of trying, the wife became pregnant and sure enough, nine months later delivered a healthy baby boy. The joyful father rushed to the nursery to see his new son. He took one look and was horrified to see the ugliest child he had ever seen.

He went to his wife and said that there was no way that he could be the father of that child. "Look at the two beautiful daughters I fathered." Then he gave her a stern look and asked, "Have you been fooling around on me?"

The wife just smiled sweetly and said, "Not this time."

Q.   How do you make your wife yell and scream during sex?

A.   Call her and tell her where you are and what you are doing!

An old farmer is outside for a walk around his land when he sees a sign on his neighbor's lawn; "Horse for Sale." Curious, he decides to have a look-see. As he approaches his neighbor's stable, he sees his old Italian friend brushing down a fine-looking stallion.

"Hello, friend, I saw your sign out there and came over to see your horse for sale." Now, the Italian farmer speaks very poor English, but manages to answer well enough. "Yep, yep, disa is da horse for-a sale."

"This horse here?" quizzes the old farmer, "Why he's a fine horse! Why-ever would you sell him?"

"Well," sighs the Italian farmer, "He no looka so good anymore."

The old farmer, convinced that his neighbor has lost his mind, makes the sale and leads the horse across his field over to the stable. As he taps the horse gently on the back to coax him into the stable, he watches as the horse misses the door completely and smacks headfirst into the wall. "That ol' cheat sold me a near blind horse!" growls the old farmer. He then proceeds to storm over across the field, reins in hand, to give his neighbor a piece of his mind. "You sold me a near blind horse, you ol' cheat, and you didn't even tell me!" he screams.

"Eh! I tolla you!" cries the Italian farmer, "I say, 'he no looka so good anymore!' "

Upon entering the little country store, the stranger noticed a sign saying "DANGER! BEWARE OF DOG!" posted on the glass door. Inside he noticed a harmless old hound dog asleep on the floor besides the cash register.

He asked the store manager, "Is THAT the dog folks are supposed to beware of?"

"Yep, that's him," he replied.

The stranger couldn't help but be amused. "That certainly doesn't look like a dangerous dog to me. Why in the world would you post that sign?"

"Because," the owner replied, "before I posted that sign, people kept tripping over him."

A police officer came upon a terrible wreck where the driver and passenger had been killed. As he looked upon the wreckage a little monkey came out of the brush and hopped around the crashed car. The officer looked down at the monkey and said, "I wish you could talk."

The monkey looked up at the officer and nodded his head up and down.

"You can understand what I'm saying?" asked the officer. Again, the monkey nodded his head up and down.

"Well, did you see this?"

"Yes," motioned the monkey.

"What happened?"

The monkey pretended to have a can in his hand and turned it up by his mouth.

"They were drinking?" asked the officer.

"Yes."

"What else?"

The monkey pinched his fingers together and held them to his mouth.

"They were smoking marijuana?"

"Yes."

"What else?"

The monkey motioned, "Screwing."

"They were screwing, too?" asked the astounded officer.

"Yes."

"Now wait, you're saying your owners were drinking, smoking and screwing before they wrecked."

"Yes."

"What were you doing during all this?"

The monkey motioned, "Driving."

"I must take every precaution not to get pregnant," said Sherri to her best friend June.

"But I thought you said your hubby had a vasectomy," June responded.

"He did. That's why I have to take every precaution!" shrieked Sherri.

A sales company has particular trouble selling Bibles. One day, a man comes in with a job application and says "I-I-I-I'd l-l-l-l-l-like t-t-t-t-to b-b-b-b- b-be a b-b-b-Bible salesman, s-s-s-sir." Initially, the manager doesn't want to give the job to this man, but decided to try him out.

After three weeks, the manager is looking at the charts and realizes that the newest guy is selling the most copies. Amazed, he calls him into his office.

"You've only worked here for three weeks and you've already sold more copies than anyone else here! How do you do it?"

"W-w-w-w-w-well, I-I g-g-g-go up t-t-t-to th-the d-d-d-door and-d-d l-l--l s-s-s-say, w-w-w-w-would y-y-y-y-y-you l-l-l-l-l-like t-t-to b-b-b-b-buy a c-c-copy o-o-of th-th-th-the b-b-b-Bible, or w-w-w-w-w-would y-y-y-y-you l-l-l-l-like m-m-me t-t-t-to r-r-r-r-read it t-t-t-t-to y-y-y-you?"

One of the best letters I ever got was from Tracie in Alaska. She wrote me about this joke:

"God Bless You!! I laughed my ass off at the joke about the stuttering Bible salesman! I used to stutter horribly and my husband could never picture me stuttering. I had him read the joke and laughed till I had tears, then told him that's exactly what I use to sound like! It was to funny. You are the Greatest! I could (and do . . .shhhh, don't tell my hubby!) spend hours on your site just reading everything. I tell everyone I know about you and send them to your site. My sis and I love your Judi awards and Dweeb letters, I just hate when she beats me to the joke and calls and tells me about it. I'm sure you may catch some flak over the joke, as you seem to over many of your jokes, but hey.....keep doing what you're doing, it's great and I know sis and I love it!!!!!"

The stockbroker was nervous about being in prison because his cellmate looked like a real thug. "Don't worry," the gruff looking fellow said, "I'm in here for a white collar crime too."

"Well, that's a relief," sighed the stockbroker. "I was sent to prison for fraud and insider trading."

"Oh, nothing fancy like that for me," grinned the convict. "I just killed a couple of priests."

An old man and woman were married for years even though they hated each other. When they had a confrontation, screams and yelling could be heard deep into the night. A constant statement was heard by the neighbors who feared the man the most. "When I die I will dig my way up and out of the grave to come back and haunt you for the rest of your life!"

They believed he practiced black magic and was responsible for missing cats and dogs, and strange sounds at all hours. He was feared and enjoyed the respect it earned him.

He died abruptly under strange circumstances and the funeral had a closed casket. After the burial, the wife went straight to the local bar and began to party as if there was no tomorrow. The gaiety of her actions was becoming extreme while her neighbors approached in a group to ask these questions: "Are you not afraid? Concerned? Worried? That this man who practiced black magic and stated when he died he would dig his way up and out of the grave to come back and haunt you for the rest of your life?"

The wife put down her drink and said, "Let the old bastard dig. I had him buried upside down."

"I can't find a cause for your illness," the doctor said. "Frankly, I think it's due to drinking."

"In that case," replied his blonde patient, "I'll come back when you are sober."

Max has a thing with shoes. He can never resist the sight of a new pair of shoes - he just has to buy them. One day Max walks by a shoe store and sees a new pair in the window. A moment later he continues his journey wearing his new shoes. When he gets home he proudly asks his wife, "Do you see something new about me?"

The wife looks at him for a moment and says, "No, dear, I can't say I do."

Max is a little pissed off, so he takes off all his clothes, except the shoes, stands in front of his wife and says, "Now look at me closely, from top to bottom, and tell me if you see anything new."

The wife looks at his hair, then his face, then lower, until she gets to his dick, which is very small and wrinkled. "There's nothing new about THAT," she says. "No, Dear, I can't say that I do."

Max gets really mad by now and hisses, "Don't you see it is looking at my NEW SHOES?!"

The wife thinks about it for a moment and suddenly her face lights up, "I suppose you should buy a new hat, then!"

The little sexy housewife was built so well the TV repairman couldn't keep his eyes off of her. Every time she came in the room, he'd near about jerk his neck right out of joint looking at her.

When he'd finished she paid him and said, "I'm going to make a . . . well . . . unusual request. But you have to first promise me you'll keep it a secret."

The repairman quickly agreed and she went on. "Well, it's kind of embarrassing to talk about, but while my husband is a kind, decent man -- sigh -- he has a certain physical weakness. A certain disability. Now, I'm a woman and you're a man . . ."

The repairman could hardly speak, "Yes, yes!"

"And since I've been wanting to ever since you came in the door . . ."

"Yes, yes!"

"Would you help me move the refrigerator?"

The waitress was waiting as patiently as she could while Amanpreet (the smartass) was dawdling over the breakfast menu. Amanpreet says, "I never return to a restaurant unless at least one of the sausages I'm served is a match in size for my own."

The waitress replies, "In that case, sir, perhaps you should take a look at the children's menu."

A site foreman had ten very lazy men working for him, so one day he decided to trick them into doing some work for a change.

"I've got a really easy job today for the laziest one among you," he announced. "Will the laziest man please put his hand up."

Nine hands went up.

"Why didn't you put your hand up?" he asked the tenth man.

"Too much trouble," came the reply.

A Kentucky teacher was quizzing her students. "Johnny, who signed the Declaration of Independence?"

He said, "Damn if I know."

She was a little put out by his swearing, so she told him to go home and to bring his father with him when he came back.

The next day, the father came with his son, and sat in the back of the room to observe.

She started back in on her quiz and finally got back to the boy. "Now, Johnny, I'll ask you again. Who signed the Declaration of Independence?"

"Well, hell, teacher," Johnny said, "I told you I didn't know."

The father jumped up in the back, pointed a stern finger at his son, and said, "Johnny, if you signed that damn thing, hell, you damn well better admit it!"

A young doctor had moved into town and was setting up a new practice. He had a new sign painted and hung in front of his office, proclaiming his specialties: "Homosexuals & Hemorrhoids."

The town fathers were upset with the sign and asked him please to change it.

The doctor was eager to please, so he put up a new sign, "Queers & Rears."

The town fathers were really fuming about that one, so they demanded that the doctor come up with a decent sign that would not offend the townspeople.

So the doctor came up with an acceptable sign, "Odds & Ends."

Back to my comments on "black jokes." "Gay" jokes fall into the same category. Everyone is so "politically correct" about it -- except the ones who are in the category that I'm making fun of.

I'm constantly amazed when I tell a joke like this and receive letters of condemnation from folks who aren't gay -- but are offended anyway. My gay readers write me and tell me what a great joke it was.

Same with the jokes about Jesus and God. I get tons of letters from the clergy in the crowd letting me know that even though they can't use the joke in their sermon on Sunday, they actually laughed at it.

One day a diver was enjoying the aquatic world 20 feet below sea level. He noticed a guy at the same depth he was, but he had on no scuba gear whatsoever.

The diver went below another 20 feet, but the guy joined him a few minutes later. The diver went below 25 feet, but minutes later, the same guy joined him. This confused the diver, so he took out a waterproof chalkboard set, and wrote, "How the heck are you able to stay under this deep without equipment?"

The guy took the board and chalk, erased what the diver had written, and wrote, "I'm drowning, you moron!"

Three nuns went to a cucumber stand in an open market one day. They asked how much the cucumbers were. The merchant said that they were four for a dollar.

The nuns agreed to purchase four. The puzzled merchant asked why they needed four cucumbers when there were only three of them.

A nun answered back, "Well, we could always eat one."

"GET ME THE FUCK OFF YOUR FUCKING LIST."

Dirk in South Africa
GET ME THE FUCK OFF YOUR FUCKING LIST

I checked, Dirk. You're not on the "Fucking List." It's a much longer list than the Joke A Day one, for one thing, and only intelligent, good-looking people are allowed there. I'm afraid you don't make the cut.

You are going to be placed on the "I'm so ignorant and ugly that I can only date sheep" listing, though.

Hu with Boeing
O.K. I was just thinking that I was going to be getting a nifty Joke a Day from you guys ...but what a service! Deep, deep within the Mailing list instructions that came with my first day on the list I read:

Q What's the cost to all of this?
A Your first born.

Q No, seriously.
A We ARE serious.

I'd like to introduce you to my "payment." His name is Benjamin. 20 years old, married once (for 5 days) ...currently chasin' the preacher's daughter. He works at Handy City here in town - 'cause when he's not trying to hawk people out of their welfare checks he can sleep in one of the big recliners in front of a TV.

He came back home about 4 months ago ...his Mama thinks that he's the sweetest thing around and his stuff don't stink. I agreed (to his coming home), as I was trying to help him get back on his feet. He'd incurred 4 grand worth of debt, which included such cuteness as him runnin' up $120 worth of penalties with the DA's in three counties for rubber checks of 2 to 5 dollars each.

He's brilliant, just ask him. It's a good thing too, 'cause I'm an idiot ...ditto on the source.

It's good that you made the offer when you did, 'cause I've been studying the efficacy of giving him the boot outta the house again. ...Ever since that momentous week a month ago that he ran up an additional $10K worth of debt. ---Bought himself a '92 Honda with 128K miles (no radio) for 7 grand (at 19% APR), and got his girl friend's (the preacher's daughter) engagement ring out of hock. ...That makes 3 engagement rings, and one wedding ring that he's currently on the payment plan for.

Every word of this is true, just tell me where to ship this piece of work, and I'll consider you my new best friend forever.

The Jokes That Started The "Judi Awards"

As you've been able to tell by reading some of the letters I've included here, there are tons of people who wound up on Joke A Day without a clue. What gets me is folks have to voluntarily sign up for the listing. They're warned before they ever get their first joke that I tell nasty jokes here. They're provided with information that tells them I think "sacred cows" make the best hamburger.

Yet, like clockwork, I can tell that I'm going to get deluged with hateful letters when I skewer someone's favorite topic.

Religion is a good incendiary topic. I can always count on Christians damning me to hell for my jokes about Jesus, and Muslims every time I mention Muhammad.

But other, seemingly innocent topics can also inspire the less mentally proficient to drop me a spiteful letter.

*The "Judi Award" is named after a blond-headed lady who didn't like one of my "blonde" jokes. She wrote to complain about it and her letter was filled with so many grammatical errors I thought she was playing a joke on **me**. Alas, she wasn't. She really was dumber than dirt.*

Throughout the years, I've taken particular joy in finding the dumbest of folks and awarding them the highest honor Joke A Day can bestow: The Judi Award.

Here are the jokes that set them off:

Judi -- June 2, 1997

There are three blondes stranded on an island. Suddenly a fairy appears and offers to grant each one of them one wish.

The first blonde asks to be intelligent. Instantly, she is turned into a brown-haired woman and she swims off the island.

The next one asks to be even more intelligent than the previous one, so instantly she is turned into a black-haired woman. The black-haired woman builds a boat and sails off the island.

The third blonde asks to become even more intelligent than the previous two. The fairy turns her into a man, and he walks across the bridge.

Jon -- July 23, 1997

The friends of the bride decided to give the newlyweds a tape recording of the couple making love on their honeymoon night as a gag wedding gift. They accomplished this by hiding a tape recorder under the newlyweds' bed that evening.

Before they gave the recorded tape to her, they played the tape and heard her moaning to her new husband, "That's happiness! That's happiness!" But her voice sounded funny and they discovered that they were playing the tape at the wrong speed.

When they slowed the tape down to the correct pitch, they were surprised to hear her shouting at him, "That's a penis?! That's a penis?!"

Amanpreet -- September 23, 1998

Armando went to his neighbor and asked, "Hey, Carlos, do you like a woman who has a beeg stomach steeking oll the way out?"

"No," says Carlos.

Armando asks, "Do you like a woman whose teets hang almost to her knees?"

"No," says Carlos.

"Well, Carlos, would you like a woman whose heeps are so mucho grande?"

"Caramba! No, amigo!" Carlos replied.

"Theen tell me why," asked Armando, "do you keep screwing my wife?"

Gayle -- December 22, 1998

Two necrophiles work in a morgue, and one of them tells the other one: "You should have seen this woman they brought in last week. They pulled her out of the water after she'd been there for three weeks. Man, I'm tellin' you, she had a clitoris just like a pickle."

"What," the other asks, "green?"

"No," says the first, "sour."

Monika -- August 14, 1999

A man sees a bumper sticker on a car in the parking lot and finds it intriguing so he goes for a closer look. The sticker reads: WWJD 69. He stands puzzling over this for awhile.

The car's female owner comes back to the car and gives the man a crafty look. The man asks her what the sticker means. He says, "I've heard of WWJD, What Would Jesus Do, but what's with the 69?"

The woman smiles and says, "Well, you know . . . '69', right?"

"Really?" The man is further intrigued.

"Yes. Well, 'WWJD 69' is 'what would Jesus taste like?'"

Letter From God

Dear Ray,

First of all, I'd like to thank you for mentioning Me from time to time. It seems most of my children have forgotten Me, or fear and despise Me because they listen to rumors instead of getting to know Me personally. Just let Me go on record here that I am, in fact, a God of LOVE. And, like all those who love, I also like to laugh.

I sent My Holy Spirit to reside in the Internet, so I'm the first to get the jokes every day. (It's a bit complicated to explain how that works, but not as complicated as that "Trinity" conspiracy theory.) The "let he who is without sin . . . " joke made Me laugh so hard, I think I blew out half a dozen Pacific islands. My Son got a kick out of it too. (He thinks like Me.)

The unfortunate part is that, after being so entertained, We then see that humans read the same joke and get mad--like it's about THEM! Well, they have their free will and can do what they want. WE know they are just jokes. Heck, I like tuna, but I don't EAT it, for Christ's sake! (ha ha) He says it makes My breath stink. (And you know how important it is for Me to have fresh breath, right?)

I don't want to take up a lot of your time, and I'm very busy myself, getting Jesus ready for the Big Day and all. But I wanted to remind you that those people who criticize you don't represent Me, and are not sent by Me (as I already said in My book.) Keep up the good work, and I will continue to bless you. Ray, We LOVE you, man!

Yours . . . truly, YHVH (a.k.a. God)

Thanks to Moonchild for writing this -- Ray

You Know You're A Joke A Day Subscriber If . . .

Before you tell your friend a joke, you ask him if he would like it in HTML format, warning him it may not come out as planned.

You think with your new-found wit you may actually be able to get with the "Babe."

Your contribution to every planning session at work is, "I know how we can get 10,000 banners for $20!"

You're the only guy who also subscribes to Learning Kingdom, Cool Word, and you got your wife one of those gold rose thingies.

You tell friends they can "unsubscribe anytime" before you tell them a joke.

Halfway through sending an email to a friend you get an urge to insert a couple of Sponsor Ads.

Two Words: Lirpa Sloof.

You think "Peanut" and "Spud" are perfectly acceptable names for children.

You realize almost everyone at work can be categorized as a "Dweeb," "Jon," or "Judi."

Joke A Day Commandments

I've read your letters section religiously ever since I stumbled on your site. Lately there's been a lot of talk about forming a religion based around Joke A Day. You could do what other sites (World Wide Recipes and Dilbert) do, and award positions in your church to the deserving. I would like a place in your church, though with my impending graduation, I fear I will lapse in faithfulness. However, to gain my position, I propose these as the church commandments:

1. Joke A Day is thy humor site. Thou shalt place none other before it, nor call it by the name of any inferior site.

2. Thou shalt freely take the names of Judi, Amanpreet, Jon, Joseph, Quint, Brian and Gayle in vain.

3. Keep holy the weekend, by reducing your workload.

4. Honor Ray as your moderator, whose standards of humor are superior to all others'.

5. Thou shalt not kill, no matter how the idiots enrage you.

6. Thou shalt not adulterate old jokes, send them to Ray, and expect them to be retold on his page, nor in his mailing.

7. Thou shalt not steal jokes from Ray without properly giving him credit.

8. Thou shalt not spread falsehoods about Joke A Day, but shall spread the word of its truth and light to the masses possessing a sense of humor.

9. Thou shalt not covet Ray's women, neither desiring his Babes, nor abiding by any slanderous thoughts against his daughters. Thou may covet his ex-wife, for verily doth he tireth of her.

10. Thou shalt not covet Ray's possessions, including his web site.

Seeing as how I've already sent at least one convert to your site and email lists, I'd ask to be in the Missionary position, but that's an unoriginal joke.   May I instead be your Minister of Education?   I envision a life of ease jetting about the world educating world leaders in the importance of humor while my underlings do the grunt work of teaching others the standards of humor in the Church of Joke A Day.

Original work by Jenn with Iowa State

My Ten Favorite Jokes

A mother, accompanied by her small daughter, was in New York City. The mother was trying to hail a cab, when her daughter noticed several wildly dressed women who were loitering on a nearby street corner. The mother finally hailed her cab and they both climbed in, at which point the daughter asks her mother, "Mummy, what are all those ladies waiting for by that corner?" to which the mother replies, "Those ladies are waiting for their husbands to come home from work."

The cabbie, upon hearing this exchange, turns to the mother and says, "Ahhhhhhh, C'mon lady!!!! Tell your daughter the truth!!!! For crying out loud. They're hookers!"

A brief period of silence follows, and the daughter then asks, "Mummy, do the ladies have any children?"

The mother replies, "Of course dear. Where do you think cabbies come from?"

A small boy is sent to bed by his father. Five minutes later:

"Da-ad..."

"What?"

"I'm thirsty. Can you bring me a drink of water?"

"No. You had your chance. Lights out."

Five minutes later: "Da-aaaad..."

"WHAT?"

"I'm THIRSTY...Can I have a drink of water??"

"I told you NO! If you ask again I'll have to spank you!!"

Five minutes later... "Daaaa-aaaad..."

"WHAT??!!"

"When you come in to spank me, can you bring me a drink of water?"

Little Johnny returns from school and says he got an F in arithmetic.

"Why?" asks the father.

"The teacher asked 'How much is 2 times 3?' I said 'six'"

"But that's right!"

"Then she asked me 'How much is 3 times 2?'"

"What's the fucking difference?"

"That's exactly what I said."

Jon and Amanpreet were in a mental institution. This place had an annual contest picking two of the best patients and giving them two questions. If they got them correct, they're deemed cured and free to go.

Jon was called into the doctor's office first and asked if he understood that he'd be free if he answered the questions correctly. The doctor said, "Jon, what would happen if I poked out one of your eyes?"

Jon said, "I'd be half blind."

"That's correct. What if I poked out both eyes?"

"I'd be completely blind." The doctor stood up, shook Jon's

hand, and told him he was free.

On Jon's way out, as the doctor filled out the paperwork, Jon mentioned the exam to Amanpreet. He told him what questions were going to be asked and gave him the answers.

So Amanpreet came in. The doctor went through the formalities and asked, "What would happen if I cut off one ear?"

Amanpreet, remembering what Jon had said was the correct answer said, "I'd be half blind."

The doctor looked a little puzzled, but went on. "What if I cut off the other ear?"

"I'd be completely blind," Amanpreet answered.

"Amanpreet, can you explain how you'd be *blind?*"

"My hat would fall down over my eyes."

One day, an Eskimo family arrived in New York City. This was the first time out of their native village, and it didn't take long before the wife got lost.

The Eskimo husband asked a passerby for help and was told to go to the police and report it.

When he got there, a police officer asked him for the wife's description.

"What's that?" asked Eskimo.

"Well, you see, a 'description' is telling what something looks like. For example, my wife is 25 years old, 5'11", weighs 140 pounds, and measures 38-25-36. Now, what can you tell me about your wife?"

"The heck with her! Let's go look for yours!"

Two gays with AIDS decide to open up a machine shop and hire only other AIDS victims. They buy a vacant lot and put up a sign announcing:

"Opening soon. Hiring now. KISS MY TOOL AND DIE SHOP."

Barbara Walters was doing a documentary on the customs of American Indians. After a tour of the reservation they were on, she asked why the difference in the number of feathers in the headdresses.

She asked a brave who had only one feather in his headdress. His reply was, "Me have only one squaw; me have only one feather."

She asked another brave, feeling the first fellow was only joking. This brave had four feathers in his headdress. He replied, "UGH, me have four feathers because me sleep with four squaws."

Still not convinced that the number of feathers indicated the number of squaws involved, she decided to interview the chief. Now the chief's headdress was full of feathers, which, needless to say, amused Ms. Walters. She asked the chief, "Why do you have so many feathers in your headdress?" The chief proudly pounded his chest and said, "Me Chief, me fuck-em all, big, small, fat, tall, me fuck-em all."

Horrified, Ms. Walters stated, "You ought to be hung."

The Chief replied, "You damned right me hung! Hung big like buffalo, long like snake."

Ms. Walters cried, "You don't have to be so goddamn hostile!

The Chief replied, "Hoss'style, dog-style, wolf-style, any-style, me fuck-em all!"

Tears in her eyes, Ms. Walters cried, "OH DEAR." The Chief said, "No Deer. Me no fuck deer. Asshole too high, and fuckers run too fast. No fuck deer."

A man went to the Doctor and the doctor tells him he has only 24 hours to live. He goes home to tell his wife and after they both had a long cry over it, he asks her if she would have sex with him because he only has 24 hours to live.

"Of course, Darling." she replies. And so they have sex.

Four hours later they are lying in bed. He turns to her again, and says, "You know I only have 20 hours to live, do you think we could do it again?"

Again she responds very sympathetically and agrees to have sex.

Another 8 hours pass. The wife had fallen asleep from exhaustion. He taps her on the shoulder, and asks her again, "You know dear, I only have 12 more hours left, how about again for old times sake?"

By this time she is getting a little annoyed, but reluctantly agrees again.

After they finish she falls back asleep. Four hours later, he taps her on the shoulder again and said, "Dear, I hate to keep bothering you but you know I only have 8 hours left before I die, can we do it one more time?"

She turns to him with a grimace on her face and says, "You know, you don't have to get up in the morning. I do!!!"

An Irishman named Murphy went to his doctor after a long illness. The doctor, after a lengthy examination, sighed and looked Murphy in the eye and said, "I've some bad news for you. You have the cancer and it can't be cured. I'd give you two weeks to a month."

Murphy, shocked and saddened by the news, but of solid character, managed to compose himself and walk from the doctor's office into the waiting room. There he saw his son, who had been waiting.

Murphy said, "Son, we Irish celebrate when things are good and celebrate when things don't go so well. In this case, things aren't so good. I have cancer and I've been given a short time to live. Let's head for the pub and have a few pints."

After three or four pints, the two were feeling a little less somber. There were some laughs and more beers. They were eventually approached by some of Murphy's old friends who asked what the two were celebrating.

Murphy told them that the Irish celebrate the good and the bad. He went on to tell them that they were drinking to his impending end. He told his friends "I've only got few weeks to live as I have been diagnosed with AIDS."

The friends gave Murphy their condolences and they had a couple more beers. After they left, Murphy's son leaned over and whispered in confusion, "Dad, I thought you said that you were dying from cancer? You just told your friends that you were dying from AIDS!"

Murphy said, "I am dying from cancer, Son. I just don't want any of them sleeping with your mother after I'm gone."

The captain called the sergeant in. "Sarge, I just got a telegram that Private Jones' mother died yesterday. Better go tell him and send him in to see me."

So the sergeant calls for his morning formation and lines up all the troops. "Listen up, men," says the sergeant. "Johnson, report to the mess hall for KP. Smith, report to Personnel to sign some papers. The rest of you men report to the Motor Pool for maintenance. Oh, by the way, Jones, your mother died. Report to the commander."

Later that day the captain called the sergeant into his office. "Hey, Sarge, that was a pretty cold way to inform Jones his mother died. Couldn't you be a bit more tactful, next time?"

"Yes, Sir," answered the sergeant.

A few months later, the captain called the sergeant in again with, "Sarge, I just got a telegram that Private McGrath's mother died. You'd better go tell him and send him in to see me. This time be more tactful."

So, the sergeant calls for his morning formation. "OK, men, fall in and listen up. Everybody with a mother, take two steps forward -- NOT SO FAST, McGRATH!"

What the Future Holds

Man, what an odyssey this book has been.

I started not long after I started Joke A Day, but on the advice of some of those afore-mentioned lawyers, I had to shelve it until some legal questions were answered.

I'm tickled it's done and I'm tickled it's in your hands.   This will certainly become an annual event.

Speaking of annual events, as of this writing in September 1999 there's plans underfoot to hold a festival every year and celebrate humor.   It'll be called Humorfest, and like Microsoft products, the name will change every year to coincide with the year of the festival.   Except we'll be more up-to-date than B. Gates and his "Borg-like" Microsoft.

So, somewhere in the summer of 2000 there'll be a great festival.   I've been talking with other Internet humor list owners, and we all think it's a pretty good idea.   Now the problem, of course, is just trying to pay for it.   That's why you should rush right back and buy another dozen copies of this book.

As of this writing Joke A Day has over 200,000 daily subscribers on one mailing list and over 100,000 subscribers on another.   I've got readers in 152 countries.   I'd sure like to see that number reach a million some day.   Things like this book will help.   Pass it along, will you?   And tell your friends to sign up for their free subscription.

I'm going to let you go now.   I appreciate you being here and thanks for taking a look-see at my book.

Ray Owens
Joke A Day

Hard at work.
Someone has to check out those "bikini" sites.

Spud. And Spud's wacky father who makes his living telling jokes on
the Internet. Yep, he's fun to bring to school on "Career Day".